The Rose Rustlers

Texas A&M AgriLife Research and Extension Service Series
Craig Nessler and Douglas L. Steele, General Editors

GREG GRANT & WILLIAM C. WELCH

Foreword by G. Michael Shoup

The Rose Rustlers

TEXAS A&M UNIVERSITY PRESS   COLLEGE STATION

This paper meets the requirements
of ANSI/NISO Z39.48-1992 (Permanence of Paper).
Binding materials have been chosen for durability.
Manufactured in China by Everbest Printing Co.,
through FCI Print Group
∞

LIBRARY OF CONGRESS CATALOGING-IN-PUBLICATION DATA

Names: Grant, Greg, 1962- author. | Welch, William C. (William Carlisle),
     1939– author.
Title: The rose rustlers / Greg Grant and William C. Welch ; foreword by
     G. Michael Shoup.
Other titles: Texas A&M AgriLife Research and Extension Service series.
Description: First edition. | College Station : Texas A&M University Press,
     [2017] | Series: Texas A&M AgriLife Research and Extension Service series
     | Includes bibliographical references and index.
Identifiers: LCCN 2016048523 (print) | LCCN 2016051147 (ebook) |
     ISBN 9781623495442 (flexbound : alk. paper) | ISBN 9781623495442 (ebook)
Subjects: LCSH: Old roses—Texas. | Old roses—Southern States. |
     Old roses—Propagation—Texas. | Rose culture—Texas. | Plant
     collecting—Southern States | Texas Rose Rustlers—History.
Classification: LCC SB411.65.O55 G74 2017 (print) | LCC SB411.65.O55 (ebook)
     | DDC 635.9/3373409764—dc23
LC record available at https://lccn.loc.gov/2016048523

COVER PHOTO: 'Farmer's Dream' (courtesy of Ralph Anderson)
BACK COVER: "Natchitoches Noisette" (courtesy of Ralph Anderson)
                     'Climbing Cramoisi Superieur' (courtesy of William C. Welch)

General editors for this series are Craig Nessler, director of Texas A&M AgriLife
Research, and Douglas L. Steele, director of the Texas A&M AgriLife Extension Service.

This book is dedicated to our late friend and Mater Rosa,
PAMELA ASHWORTH PURYEAR (1943–2005).
Without her dogged curiosity, Texas-sized vision,
and boundless enthusiasm, the Texas Rose Rustlers,
the Antique Rose Emporium, and this book would
never have existed. There will never be another like her.
Not even close.

When I was studying horticulture in the Brazos Valley at Texas A&M University, in the 1980s, my mentor Bill Welch introduced me to the most fascinating person imaginable, like someone from a Roald Dahl children's book. I met her on the front porch of the once-grand two-story home her great-grandfather built in sleepy Navasota, Texas, during an early meeting of the famed Texas Rose Rustlers. Her unforgettable name was Pamela Ashworth Puryear, and she lived with her elderly mother, Missy (Laura). They both had slow Southern drawls that flowed like ribbon cane syrup on a frosty morning. Pam was a historian, genealogist, artist, calligrapher, and self-proclaimed *Princess*. She was undoubtedly the most eccentric person I've ever met, and that's saying something, as I'm not exactly normal myself and collect unconventional friends like marigolds collect mites.

Pam Puryear and Bill Welch rustle a red China rose in a San Antonio cemetery.

As the purported first female graduate student at Texas A&M University, Pam took me under her wing and indoctrinated me in the fields of heirloom plants, historical Southern nurseries, and early Texas horticulturists—along with hundreds of other subjects. Dearest "Aunty Pam" would have done anything in the world for me.

Pam was very interested in *every* aspect of my life and wrote me hundreds of letters,

The many letters Pam wrote to Greg cover myriad topics including horticulture, history, and house restoration.

most of which I've saved. As I read the first few I remember thinking how amazing they were and wanting to save them to publish as a book of their own one day. Bill and others have always cringed at the thought of this, because Pam named names! Why should they be embarrassed? I'm the one she wanted to paint in the nude!

She wrote in a free-flowing Victorian style with topics fluctuating between horticulture, genealogy, Texas history (Sam Houston and Texas Independence Day were favorites), the latest local "social" escapades, and my dream of restoring my grandparents' old dogtrot house. She often wrote my mother as well. Unfortunately, my poor mom couldn't make "head nor tail" of the letters. Many of mine were composed over several days and shifted gears several times. Other times she might write me three letters during the same week. Reading a Pam letter was like staring into a painting that both Monet and Picasso worked on together. She might quote Aristotle and the Bible while channeling the local dead, all in the same letter. Most contained foot-notes, references, and additional materials crammed into the margins. And once a year a big package would arrive with one of her signature oversized homemade Victorian valentines complete with ribbons and bows. She was always fabricating something for me—cushions, vests, painted T-shirts, signs, family crests, botanical art, and so forth. She also regularly tossed in seeds, snapshots or slides of plants, magazine clippings, or occasionally entire books.

Pam unfortunately passed away in 2005 but certainly left a lasting impact on me, Bill, and the world of Texas horticulture. After all, she was one of the three founding members of the Texas Rose Rustlers. Without the Rose Rustlers, there's a good chance there never would have been an Antique Rose Emporium in Independence, Texas. And without Dr. Welch's involvement with the Antique Rose Emporium and my working there in its infant stages, there's a decent chance that I'd be landscaping with red-tipped photinia, Asian jasmine, and waxleaf ligustrum topiaries to this day. My life, house, and garden wouldn't be the same without Pam. Our world of roses wouldn't be the same without her, either.

— GREG GRANT

CONTENTS

FOREWORD

Who doesn't love stories about the discovery of heirloom plants? Wherever botany, history, and humans meet, fascinating landscapes unfold.

With *The Rose Rustlers*, Dr. William "Bill" Welch and Greg Grant offer a wonderfully personal, in-depth, and entertaining account of some of the great stories gathered during their years as participants in one of the most important plant-hunting efforts of the twentieth century—the quest to save antique roses that disappeared from the market in a notoriously trend-driven business. Their experiences and friendships with other figures of the heirloom rose world bring an insider's perspective to lore first introduced in such classics of garden writing as Tom Christopher's *In Search of Lost Roses* and Steve Bender, Felder Rushing, and Allen Lacy's *Passalong Plants*.

No one in the past forty-five years has so profoundly impacted Texas horticulture as Bill Welch, who has spent many years with the Texas A&M AgriLife Extension Service. He helped develop the state's Master Gardener program. His lectures on perennials, roses, and landscape design have been heard by almost every Master Gardener training class in Texas. He has presented his landscape design courses twice a year since 1972. With a tireless work ethic, he has also written numerous books and given hundreds of talks at garden clubs and other meetings across the South.

Many leaders of Southern horticulture have benefited from Bill's expertise, but I feel especially lucky to have worked with him firsthand when we started the Antique Rose Emporium in 1982. Under his tutelage, I learned the value of roses as useful landscape plants. Numerous varieties that we reintroduced to commerce continue to blossom across the emporium's eight acres. Over a thirty-year stretch, they have enchanted thousands of visitors with an "ooh and aah" experience. Bill knew that potential when he rustled his first rose.

Greg, too, is a Texas treasure. With keen powers of observation and a gentle voice, he shares a passion for gardening that is beautifully apparent in this book. At the risk of sounding cheeky, I'll also call him a plant whisperer. In Greg's presence, plants reveal amazing ranges of expression. He has discovered not only new species but also color mutations on many flowers, as well as climbing forms of shrubs. His foundlings and introductions have dramatically broadened the palette for Southern gardens. Greg has reconstructed old buildings and earlier plantings that represent typical East Texas settings.

Greg also understands the significance of plants within the history of human culture, making him an eloquent spokesperson for the preservation of heirloom plants. While the phrase "rose rustling" may suggest an Old West–style plant heist, searching for and rescuing nostalgic old roses is actually an honorable undertaking. There is etiquette involved in their acquisition, without any pulling of guns.

Many rustled roses have withstood tests of time and Mother Nature, surviving decades without proper care through droughts and blue northers before being rescued by keen-eyed plant enthusiasts. They have undergone a natural process of selection.

Among them are several "found" or "mystery" roses such as "Maggie," "Mary Minor," and "Old Gay Hill Cemetery Red," the names of which reflect something about the place they were salvaged or the gardener who shared

Martha Gonzales's cottage garden in Navasota, Texas, featured the small red China rose given the study name "Martha Gonzales" along with 'Old Blush,' a rose in cultivation for possibly more than a thousand years.

them. The early rustlers mined old cemeteries where hardy roses were planted long ago to honor loved ones who once adored their flowers. They also traipsed politely into the small-town yards of green-thumbed gardeners who generously shared cuttings from plants that were often passed down from their mothers and grandmothers.

In *The Rose Rustlers*, Bill and Greg also introduce us to some of the original Texas Rose Rustlers, including Pam Puryear, Margaret Sharpe, and Joe Woodard. Intrepid spirits who were never shy about approaching a rose, no matter where it resided, these twentieth-century pioneers made the rescue business lively and fun. I wish they were still around to see all the magic that took root.

In his 1943 novella *The Little Prince*, Antoine de Saint-Exupéry suggests, "It is the time you have wasted on a rose that makes it so valuable." I can see his point; we instinctively want to coddle these wonderful plants. But I'm sure Bill and Greg would agree with me that no time spent with heirloom roses is wasted.

Antique roses bring something special to our lives. They deserve to be saved and shared, along with their stories. Grow them—revel in the pleasure of their fragrance and their heady histories—and your own garden memories are sure to flourish.

—G. MICHAEL SHOUP

NOTES ON QUOTES

You will notice in this book that we have used single quotes for some rose names, double quotes for others, and occasionally no quotes at all. What gives? Though it may seem a little confusing at first glance, the explanation is fairly simple. Rose names with single quotes are true named cultivars, recognized throughout the world by their exact identity. Cultivars in single quotes have been used in botanical taxonomy for many years now. It simply means that this is the rose's "real" name. Cultivar names in single quotes are always capitalized.

When we've used double quotes around a rose's name, that means it's just a study name, or a nickname if you will, because the rose's true identity or real name isn't known. Unfortunately, many antique roses go back a hundred years or more to when photography wasn't used in garden books and nursery catalogs. And because roses are the most popular flower in the world, this means there are hundreds and hundreds of similar descriptions for roses no longer in commerce or cultivation. Some roses, like 'Cecile Brunner,' 'Mutabilis,' and 'Duchesse de Brabant,' were distinct and popular enough that nobody ever forgot their names. However, the majority of lost and rustled roses may never find their true names again and may keep their double-quote study names for as long as they stay in cultivation the second time around. Unfortunately, the same rose may end up with multiple study names depending on where and by whom they are found. One example is my "Big Momma's Blush" from my great-grandmother's old home place in East Texas, as it appears to be the same rose that Ruth Knopf found and introduced as "Rock Hill Peach Tea" in South Carolina. In the early days of the Texas Rose Rustlers I even remember another found rose with three different names.

In addition, you will notice that sometimes we don't have any quotes at all around a rose name. These are common names for popular roses like the butterfly rose, the sweetheart rose, and the green rose. There have never been rules for using common names, and some plants have more than one common name.

And finally, in the modern nursery world, roses will generally have nonsensical cultivar names in single quotes along with designated trademark names used for marketing.

I apologize for all the mess, but I didn't make it! Just remember Shakespeare's words: "What's in a name? That which we call a rose by any other name would smell as sweet."

—GREG GRANT

INTRODUCTION

The way I see it, a rose ought to exist to please the grower, not vice versa!

— PAMELA ASHWORTH PURYEAR

Rose rustling is nothing new; for as long as there have been roses, there have been those seeking them out. Famed and witty newspaper columnist Leon Hale described the phenomenon of rose rustling in perhaps the best language in a 1982 feature he wrote for the *Houston Post*:

> What rose rustling means, it means you go out and find old rose bushes blooming in isolated places. Roses that you can't buy any longer but have survived around country houses and grown-up fence rows and the like. And you take cuttings and try to make the roses bloom and search in old seed catalogues and look for identifications. Lot of people interested in that now, it seems—going out and rustling old roses.

Many of the old roses found today in the American South were bred in Europe and were initially grown by the royal and the wealthy. The queen of rose rustling must surely have been Empress Josephine, first wife of Napoleon Bonaparte. After all, she strived to have every rose in the world growing in her garden at Malmaison, near Paris. It is even reported that wars were paused while ships carrying her new finds passed through. Rose buffs like us can be thankful that she had Pierre-Joseph Redouté paint a number of them. He went on to publish his famous *Les Roses* (1817–1820), which featured around 75 of her Malmaison roses in its 168 plates.

Antique roses made their way from Europe to the American South via botanical gardens and fine nurseries and then into wealthy plantations and city gardens. Then, as newer roses were developed and became all the rage, the most popular of the older ones filtered down into the hands of the common people, who ultimately shared them with their kin and friends. This

A 150-year-old specimen of 'Old Blush' in New Braunfels, Texas.

eventually brought them to farmhouses and rural cemeteries, where a precious few managed to survive into the twentieth century.

Throughout the 1980s, a small band of Texans scouted these rural homesites, abandoned places, and cemeteries searching for forgotten roses. We called ourselves the Texas Rose Rustlers, but we were far from outlaws. The name belied our lofty intent and sense of decorum. "Always ask for permission" and "Never desecrate the site of a found rose" were cardinal rules. To preserve raw, fragrant beauty and resilience, with repeat blooming as a bonus, was the aim. Exasperation with the hybrid tea roses popular at the time fueled our purpose. Most gardeners were fussing with hybrid teas and failing miserably, achieving at most a single large bloom at the top of short, stick-like branches. To control black spot and mildew, it was necessary to spray weekly during the growing season. Most of these modern roses were weak growers grafted onto a vigorous rootstock. They lacked fragrance along with vigor, drought tolerance, and general worthiness.

This hybrid tea style of flower was about all that was available. Roses were most often planted in separate beds and grown intensively for cut flowers. The large, rounded shrubs, billowy climbers on fences and pergolas, compact hedges, and graceful accent roses of earlier cottage gardens were becoming a distant memory. For this reason, Pamela Puryear looked twice one August when she spied a rose "blooming its head off." It was a blistering hot and dry summer in south-central Texas, but despite being obviously neglected, the rose flourished beside an old log house. Pamela's cuttings of this bush, which she dubbed her "pioneer rose," rooted easily and launched a newfound passion.

Pam Puryear was the mastermind and definite dominant personality among the folks she recruited in 1982 to form the Texas Rose Rustlers, formally a regional affiliate of the national Heritage Roses Group. Created in 1975, the Heritage Roses Group, according to its website, is "a fellowship of those who care about old garden roses, species roses, old or unusual roses— particularly those roses introduced into commerce prior to the year 1867. Its purposes are to preserve, enjoy, and share knowledge about the old roses." All of Pam's first recruits adopted this assignment with enthusiasm. In an article published in *Country America* in April 1992, Pam listed the essentials for an old rose rustle:

> All that is really needed for rustling old roses are sharp pruning shears, plenty of insect repellent, a sure cure for poison ivy, stout boots, some dollar bills, an honest-seeming face, the words for "friend" and "don't shoot" in several languages, plastic bags, a supply of willow water, someone to drive the getaway car and a Sense of Mission.

"This last is a polite term for the complete obsession that afflicts old rose collectors," she added.

In these pages, we attempt to chronicle our origins, adventures, and discoveries as Texas Rose Rustlers. When we met in the Horticulture Department at Texas A&M University, we immediately recognized each other as kindred spirits who shared a lifelong quest for beauty, an affinity for heirlooms, and a drive to educate. Here we present tales—some long, some short, and some tall—of the many efforts that have helped restore lost roses to not only residential gardens, but also commercial and church landscapes in Texas.

NOTED ROSE RUSTLERS

Greg Grant

*I*f the queen of rose rustling was Empress Josephine, the king most
certainly was Robert Fortune, perhaps the most accomplished plant
rustler of all time. Fortune was a Scottish-born horticulturist who
collected for what is now the Royal Horticultural Society and later
served as the curator of the famous Chelsea Physic Garden. Between 1843
and 1862, Robert Fortune explored the botanical riches of China and Japan
and introduced around 120 new species and varieties of plants to horticulture
and botany. *Rosa × fortuniana*, Fortune's double yellow; *Rosa anemoniflora*, a
double-flowered purple rugosa rose; and the now-lost Fortune's five colored
rose were among these spoils.

Southern horticulture can also thank him for a multitude of other classics
including popcorn spirea, kumquat, abelia, winter honeysuckle, double-
flowered peaches, flowering almond,
pearl bush, Confederate jasmine,
Chinese fringe tree, Japanese anemo-
nes, and a number of camellias and
azaleas.

In modern times, rose rustling
has pretty much been divided up
into three factions—the Californians,
the East Coast contingency, and the
Texans.

California

In California, Fred Boutin has spent
over forty years collecting and identifying old roses. A hedge of the then
unidentified 1842 hybrid perpetual
'La Reine,' which he passed by daily

Robert Fortune's
introduction to
the west, *Rosa ×
fortuniana*, adorns
a gate to a field at
Cricket Court.

The Hollywood Cemetery in Richmond, Virginia.

on his bicycle in college, was the catalyst that led him into the world of antique roses. He would later serve as botanist at the famed Huntington Botanical Gardens, where he greatly expanded the library's collection of rose books, catalogs, and heirloom roses.

Gregg Lowery got so involved in old roses that he founded Vintage Gardens, a former Sebastopol mail-order nursery specializing in an incredible array of antique roses. For a number of years he also served as the vice president of publications for the Heritage Rose Foundation and was a contributor to *Noisette Roses: 19th Century Charleston's Gift to the World* and *Mystery Roses around the World*. He now serves as the garden curator for the Friends of Vintage Gardens.

While working at Korbel Winery in Northern California, Phillip Robinson uncovered a number of old roses while redoing an area around an 1800s-era cottage on the property. This was all it took to direct him into a lifetime of searching out, identifying, and speaking about antique roses.

Sisters Joyce Demits and Virginia Hopper have also spent their life in search of lost roses. Beginning in the mid-1960s, they searched on horseback for lost treasures in old homesites in the area. Mendocino County turned out to be a hotbed of interesting mystery roses. In 1981 they opened Heritage Rose Gardens nursery, which was in business until the late 1990s and offered their interesting unknown roses along with many others. In 1975 they were founding members of the Heritage Roses Group. They made large donations of roses to the San Jose Heritage Rose Garden and were instrumental in creating a display garden of Mendocino County found roses at the Mendocino Coast Botanical Gardens in Fort Bragg. They were also nice enough to share a number of their interesting found China roses with me.

East Coast

The older gardens of the East Coast have always fostered interest in rediscovering and growing antique roses. And no one was ever more interested in wrestling with the identification of mystery roses than the late Leonie Bell. From the 1950s to the 1980s, Mrs. Bell tackled mystery after mystery from old homesites and cemeteries. Bell used a systematic approach in attempting to identify lost roses by writing detailed descriptions of the plants and their locations, sketching their floral parts, researching books and articles, and checking existing named collections. She was inspired by Mrs. Frederick Love Keays, who wrote about collecting old roses in the mid-Atlantic states in the *American Rose Annual* from 1932 to 1946.

Marie Butler searched for and collected roses from historical sites throughout her native Virginia with her late husband, John. She, her husband, and Charles Walker are credited with rediscovering the musk rose (*Rosa moschata*) on the Crenshaw plot in Richmond's historical Hollywood Cemetery. In 1995 Marie and John served as consultants for the refurbished "Virginia House" Tea Rose Garden for the Virginia Historical Society in Richmond.

Though I never had the pleasure of meeting Bell or Butler, I was very much honored to know South Carolina's Ruth Knopf. As the wife of a Baptist minister, she discovered care-free roses and other heirloom plants blooming in the nearby Rock Hill Cemetery. In the 1970s she began a garden around the parsonage consisting of exuberant tea and China roses she had admired, collected, and propagated. Her enthusiasm didn't stop with roses, as her South Carolina cottage garden overflowed with old-fashioned perennials and bulbs as well.

Inspired by Raleigh rosarian Carl Cato and an assortment of books on old roses, Miss Ruth was officially smitten. Sadly, after the sudden death of her husband she was forced to move out of the parsonage and had to endure the swift destruction of her beautiful garden. Fortunately, she shared cuttings of her roses and other pass-along finds with friends around the country and was able to plant many of them in her new beachside garden on Sullivan's Island, near Charleston.

Charleston was the home of the original Noisette rose, so naturally many of the plants Ruth collected turned out to be Noisettes and their kin. Noisette roses became the only class of roses originating in America when, around 1802, South Carolina rice farmer John Champneys produced a hybrid of 'Old Blush' and *Rosa moschata*, creating 'Champneys' Pink Cluster,' which

Southern rose rustler extraordinaire Ruth Knopf at Boone Hall Plantation in Mount Pleasant, South Carolina.

he shared with his botanist neighbor Philippe Noisette, who in turn shared it or seeds of it with his nurseryman brother Louis in France. Louis further developed the class by creating more hybrids and sharing them with the nursery and gardening world. Because of their Southern roots, many Noisette roses have been rediscovered still thriving throughout the Gulf Coast region.

Ruth went on to become a champion of Noisette roses, pointing out that these historical treasures were supremely adapted for Southern climes. After attending the first conference on antique roses at the Huntington Botanical Gardens in California, she went on to organize Charleston's International Heritage Rose Conference in 2001, where I had the privilege of speaking on China roses.

In addition, she helped form the Noisette Trail in Charleston, orchestrated the planting of the Noisette Study Garden in Hampton Park, and amassed an amazing collection of teas, Chinas, Noisettes, and other old South Carolina roses and plants at Boone Hall Plantation, which I had the pleasure of visiting. One of the many plants we grew at the SFA Mast Arboretum in Nacogdoches, Texas, was her "quill flowered" 'Miss Caroline,' which she named for her daughter. She found this spontaneous narrow-petaled sport on a branch of 'Duchesse de Brabant.' The South has never known a sweeter, more dedicated rosarian than dear Ruth Knopf.

Texas

Texas was a little late to jump on the rose-rustling bandwagon, but the three who finally kicked it off in 1982 were Pam Puryear, Margaret Sharpe, and Bill Welch.

Bill Welch sniffs
out a surviving
tea rose in a San
Antonio cemetery.

Pam Puryear was the mother of all rose rustling in Texas. Pam loved finding and sharing both treasures and stories. What she lacked in organizational
skills, she more than made up for with enthusiasm, entertainment, and Texas
bravado. She made the Texas Rose Rustlers a legend. And while Pam beat the
bushes and briars like a possessed porcus after truffles, Margaret Sharpe, a
modern rose enthusiast from Houston who grew into old garden roses, provided leadership and organization to this new group of rosarians gone wild.

Pam and Margaret brought Bill and his PhD into the fold to lend cred-
ibility to the cause, and that he did. In addition to being prolific at sniffing out
lost roses, he demonstrated how to create beautiful landscapes using these
living antiques. Prior to Bill's influence, most Southern home rose gardens
generally comprised assorted gangly hybrid teas hidden in separate beds in
the backyard.

Another member who joined the antique rose cause was Cleo Barnwell
of Shreveport, Louisiana. She was born in Texas and never forgot it! She
divided her heart between the causes of wildflowers, heirloom bulbs, and
old-fashioned roses. Cleo had a wonderful Southern garden library and was
friends with the legendary Louisiana naturalist, artist, and horticulturist Caroline Dorman. Cleo Barnwell lived for one hundred flower-filled years. Her
husband once said, "Cleo, since I've started traveling with you, I think we go
more in reverse than we go forward!" According to fellow rose rustler Mitzi

VanSant, Cleo wasn't happy with the moniker "rose rustler," as it implied something illegal. As a Native Texan, Cleo was of course more familiar with cattle rustling!

Mitzi VanSant grew up in Washington State and gardened from the time she was in the fifth grade. In 1974 she read Louise Beebe Wilder's *The Fragrant Garden* (1932) and was forever changed by the sixth chapter, "Odours of the Rose." After searching for old roses in her hometown of Seattle, she moved to Austin in 1979. Then after trips to the legendary rose havens of England; Tyler, Texas; and Shreveport, Louisiana, she officially became an avid rosarian. Around 1982 she attended a meeting of other enthusiasts of old garden roses at the American Rose Society headquarters in Shreveport, where she met heavyweights Joe Woodard, Margaret Sharpe, Bill Welch, Pam Puryear, and Cleo Barnwell. Her fate was sealed. As lovers of all flowers scented, Mitzi and Cleo would remain good friends for the next thirty years. Mitzi says, "What I learned from Cleo Barnwell and memories from my great-grandmother's garden inspired me to become a passionate gardener and later landscape designer, and to create the Smithville [Texas] cottage garden that I now tend."

After joining the Texas Rose Rustlers, Mitzi became the Austin contact for the group and eventually a commissioned sales rep for Mike Shoup and Bill Welch's Antique Rose Emporium, visiting nurseries in Austin and San Antonio and getting them to carry the plants in their retail nurseries.

She also created a beautiful cul-de-sac garden full of old-fashioned roses on Evans Avenue in Austin. She started collecting old roses from all the usual sources, including Roses of Yesterday and Today in California and Hortico and Pickering Nurseries, both in Canada. At one point, she had more than 120 different varieties of old roses, including many once-blooming varieties. Later, upon gaining some experience, Mitzi culled out most of the old European roses that mildewed and got black spot and went on to collect more of the more Southern-adapted teas, Chinas, Bourbons, Noisettes, and hybrid musks, which bloomed almost constantly. Her rose collection got so large that it spilled out into the traffic circle in front of the house. The garden featured a large specimen of 'Mermaid' trained around the bottom of and then up into a large pecan tree in the front yard, along with a beautiful specimen of 'Climbing Etoile de Hollande' that covered the entire east side of the house. Mitzi also had a large plant of 'Madame Alfred Carriere' trained on the front porch railing, and 'May Queen' on a wooden trellis nailed to the side of the small white garden shed in the backyard.

The traffic circle had many large shrubs such as 'Blush Noisette,' 'General Jacqueminot,' and another 'Mermaid' that was trained up and over a fishing net hanging from a guy wire that supported a telephone pole.

Sadly, many noted rose rustlers have passed on. But as long as gardeners plant roses and leave them behind, there will always be rustling to do. In these days of migration to cities, urban sprawl, and per-petual-care cemeter-ies, there are precious heirloom roses still to

The late Cleo Barnwell stands in a magical planting of naturalized *Narcissus* in a North Louisiana garden.

be saved. Some may be hacked to the ground next to tombstones. Others may be hidden in fencerows. And still others may be next to dilapidated homes along country roads. My dad even talks about rambling pink "wild roses" he mows to the ground each year at an old homesite in the middle of a pasture. It really doesn't matter whether the roses are old or famous. What matters is that they are still alive. Precious heirloom roses deserve to be rescued and saved just as much as priceless furniture and antique jewelry.

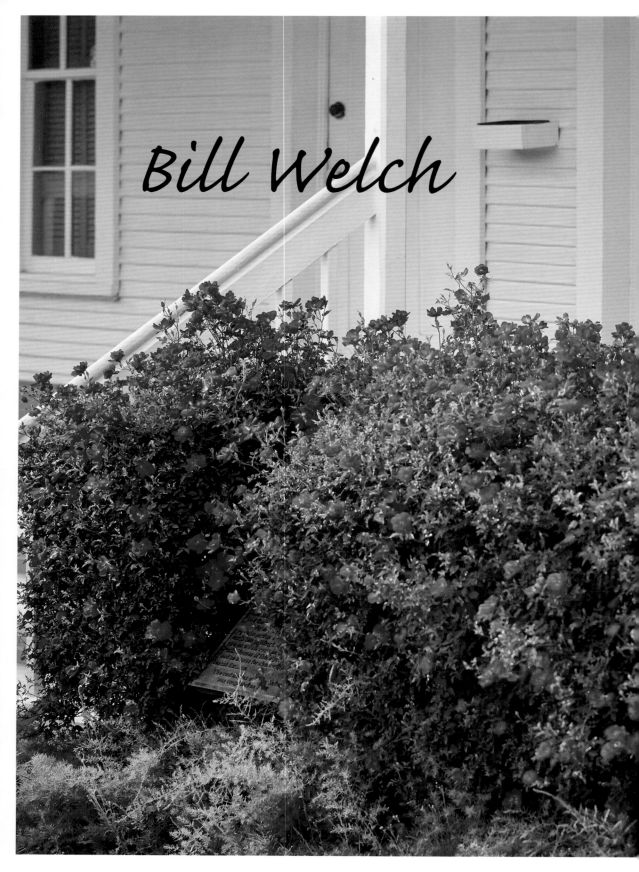
Bill Welch

GROWING INTO A ROSARIAN

My interest in roses began when I was about nine years old. My mother had a modest rose garden at our home in the Garden Oaks area of Houston, where she and my dad had built a new house the year I was born (1939). The rose bed was anchored on one end by a large freestanding specimen of 'Paul's Scarlet' that put on quite a display each spring. About ten various hybrid teas of the period, such as 'Talisman,' 'Chrysler Imperial,' and 'Eclipse,' were struggling to survive. Early one summer the June bugs attacked the rose foliage with a vengeance, and I was fascinated with them. My mother decided that one way to control the pests was to induce me to catch them. She offered a nickel per June bug, and I immediately went to work capturing them and putting them in a fruit jar. She hadn't planned on the number I harvested and became concerned when my numbers reached the hundreds and she had to dispense more nickels than she had anticipated.

In September 1952 we moved into a new home in the Briarcroft subdivision in the Galleria area of Houston. The Garden Oaks home had been located in a Pineywoods part of Houston with sandy soil, but the new one was in sticky black gumbo. It clung to our shoes and had to be scraped off with shovels and hoes to keep them operational. I was thirteen years old and in the ninth grade when I began working at Paul's Green Thumb Nursery on weekends, and I continued there most weekends through high school. I was fascinated with the world of plants and enjoyed waiting on customers and learning about plants and gardening practices from them. Tyler roses were a big part of the business; bare-root plants arrived in big boxes in January and were potted into containers for sale almost immediately. Many roses were also marketed in packages with the tops dipped in paraffin to keep them from drying out.

I was given the opportunity to landscape our new house and I wanted roses to be a significant part of the plan. At the time, floribunda roses were the rage, and I selected salmon-pink 'Fashion' (Boerner, 1949), 'Pink Rosette' (Krebs, 1948), orangey-red 'Floradora' (Tantau, 1944) and pink 'Ma Perkins' (Boerner, 1952) to mass at the ends of a long bed that spanned most of the width of the backyard. They did quite well and I was fascinated with the fact that they were budded onto a completely different rootstock. I asked Paul Robinson, owner of Paul's Green Thumb Nursery and, later, a mentor and friend, why roses were grafted. He explained that the understock made the plants more vigorous and that "modern roses" just didn't grow well from cuttings. Sure enough, after two or three years, my newly set-out roses began to suffer from black spot and lose their vigor.

The story was different with the roses my grandmother and aunts were growing from cuttings of slips gathered from friends and family. My Aunt Edna was a good gardener and lived in a rock house in Rosenberg, Texas. Next-door neighbors Mr. and Mrs. Fisher were excellent gardeners and had lots of roses I later learned were 'Old Blush.' The individual flowers were relatively small but occurred most of the year, and the plants were healthy. The Fishers rooted their plants from cuttings and shared some with Aunt Edna, who was familiar with 'Old Blush,' which was grown by her grandparents on their farm near Yoakum, Texas. I still drive by Aunt Edna's home on Carlisle Street when I pass through to teach Fort Bend Master Gardener classes, and

Aunt Edna Koym's house, Rosenberg, Texas.

some of the 'Old Blush' roses she planted in the late 1940s are still thriving. In her side yard she had alternated 'Old Blush' with bridal wreath (*Spiraea cantoniensis*) because it reminded her of a big bouquet when both bloomed simultaneously in April and May.

My Grandmother Menke had a pleasant white farmhouse on 120 acres at the edge of Yoakum. It was on top of a hill with a rather formal planting of hackberry trees around the perimeter, which was fenced with white painted posts and hoop wire. My grandfather painted the hackberry trunks white. Although it was before my time, Grandmother Menke spoke enthusiastically about a nice specimen of 'Marechal Niel' rose (1864, Pradel) planted on a trellis in front of a west-facing bay window. She also had beautiful crape-myrtles, crinums, and paperwhite narcissus. 'Old Blush' and pink 'Eugene Boerner' roses dotted the swept areas as well as fragrant gardenias and hydrangeas. During my lifetime, her front yard was planted in St. Augustine-grass, but both sides of the house still retained remnants of a swept garden.

Grandmother Menke taught me to root plants in rainwater. When I was eight or nine years old, she showed me how to take gardenia cuttings and place them in rainwater inside a fruit jar. She then left the cuttings on a bench that was partially shaded. I was amazed when the cuttings sprouted

When he was eight years old, Bill's Grandmother Menke taught him how to root gardenia cuttings in a fruit jar filled with rainwater.

roots several weeks later. My Grandmother Welch also lived in Yoakum and was known for her huge specimen of double pink althea, pots of geraniums, and masses of blue plumbago at the foot of her large front porch. Cuttings from her althea were shared with all our family as well as many friends. I am wishing for a cutting of it right now!

I was undecided what to do when I graduated from Lamar High School in 1957. A family friend suggested Southwestern University at Georgetown, Texas, and I chose to major in business administration. I loved Georgetown and the university, but by the time I entered my second year I knew I needed to get into something more specifically in line with my interests.

In early January 1959 I wrote to Dr. Robert Reich, head of the Landscape Architecture Department at Louisiana State University (LSU). I also contacted Professor Robert White, Landscape Architecture head at Texas A&M. At that time, Texas A&M was a male military school. Dr. Reich responded immediately and told me to come there right away. I told him I had to finish the semester but would come for a seminar he was having in June. The Landscape Architecture Program was fairly large at LSU but was a community within the university. Dr. Reich introduced me to Dr. Neil Odenwald, who was looking for someone to share an apartment with, and I entered in the fall of 1959. Neil and I have been coauthors and remain lifelong friends.

Dr. Reich's interests were very modern, and Garrett Eckbo and Thomas

Church were our favorite famous landscape architects. He taught the plant materials courses with an assistant and we visited neighborhoods close to the campus for collecting and viewing materials. "Doc" was famous for his "running tests" in which he would scramble us through neighborhoods and point to a plant and we would be expected to produce the correct scientific name. Dr. Reich was a challenging teacher but had a way of relating to his students and encouraging them. We were all expected to accept summer jobs that were "far and wide." I chose to go to Hawaii and work for Richard Tongg, a famous Chinese landscape architect with offices in Waikiki.

I was able to complete the normal five-year program at LSU in three years. In 1962, I graduated with a degree in landscape architecture and spent six months of active duty in the army at Fort Polk, Louisiana. Afterward, I went to work for the landscape department of Cornelius Nurseries in Houston. Within a year, I had an opportunity to work in partnership with Lynn Lowrey, whom I had known for years and for whom I had great respect as a native plant authority and outstanding horticulturist. I first met nurseryman and plant explorer Lynn Lowrey as a teenager in Houston. He was a graduate of the horticulture program at LSU and grew up in Many, Louisiana. Lynn had become very interested in native plants of Texas and Mexico. Lowrey Nursery introduced for the first time many of the native plants we see in Houston. He had a loyal following of influential Houstonians who loved plants, and he encouraged them to experiment with them in their landscapes. Lynn was well aware of good landscape architecture and worked with the leading professionals in Houston such as Robert White, Fred Buxton, Ralph Gunn, C. C. Pat Fleming, Ruth London, and others. He was committed, however, to encouraging Houstonians to develop naturalistic islands of native plants as part of their gardens.

My time with Lynn helped shape my interest in tough, hardy, and sustainable plants. He introduced me to anaqua trees (Ehretia anacua), interesting Mexican oaks (Quercus spp.), wild olives (Cordia boissieri), orchid trees (Bauhinia congesta), and Texas sages (Leucophyllum spp.). Perennial favorites included Salvia greggii, both yellow and red columbines (Aquilegia spp.), Brazos penstemon (Penstemon tenuis), and various rain lilies (Zephyranthes, etc.). During that time, we did landscape work for an interesting clientele of Houstonians, and I learned a great deal about the role of native and adapted plants.

Two years into that experience, I received an invitation to return to LSU for graduate school and half-time employment as extension landscape horti-

Lynn Lowrey, Houston nurseryman who first introduced many Mexican and native plants to Texas gardeners.

culturist there. I spent several years working on my master's and doctorate at LSU. During that time I met Diane Thames, who was a child development specialist with the Louisiana Department of Education. Diane and I married in December 1967, and she was most supportive of my career and education. She had a host of friends who provided many years of encouragement.

There were few sources of old roses during the early days of our interest. Sharing with friends, neighbors, and relatives was about the only way of obtaining these roses, and many times they didn't have "true names." Among the earliest sources were Roses of Yesterday and Today in California and Pickering Nursery in Ontario, Canada. Mr. Shraven at Pickering had an extensive collection of old roses and was able to ship them all over the United States. Fred Edmonds and Roy Hennessey of Scappoose, Oregon, also had large catalog collections.

My rose-rustler friend and horticulture colleague Cynthia Mueller purchased twenty or so old favorites from Roy Hennessey and planted them where she lived below San Antonio, Texas, in the 1960s. After a flood with standing water killed almost all of them, she wrote to Roy about what had happened. In return came a bundle of bare-root substitutions, with no bill— an act of kindness from a crusty old nurseryman that she never forgot. The entire cost of postage was only $2.96. She wrote a letter of thanks, and it was returned by the post office as "addressee deceased."

THE TEXAS ROSE RUSTLERS

*I*n February 1972, an exciting move brought Diane and me to Texas A&M University, where I accepted a position as landscape horticulture specialist for the Texas Agricultural Extension Service. As I traveled around Texas talking to homeowners, nurserymen, and garden professionals, I began to realize even more that many modern American plants were not very well suited to our conditions. However, I could see in old gardens and homesites beautiful plants that had endured for generations with little attention. These old-fashioned beauties were often difficult to find commercially. I began to wonder whether some of the best of these could be propagated and reintroduced to the gardening public. Among the most obvious choices were old roses that showed great promise as landscape plants in all parts of the garden. Vines, billowing shrubs, hedges, and specimens were all present, sometimes completely nameless.

A few years after moving to College Station, Diane and I decided we would like to have a weekend home in nearby Washington County. I was ready for a Texas country garden with some old roses and perennials. It was here that I planted my earliest antique rose collection at a turn-of-the-twentieth-century cottage. Sixteen of the early Texas Rose Rustlers met at

Rose Rustlers at Rehburg, 1982.

this Rehburg home and garden in late 1982. Pam Puryear, secretary, asked me to serve as president of the fledgling organization. I had first met Pam when she made an appointment and came to visit me in my office at Texas A&M. She knew of my interest in roses and other ornamentals and was sure I'd be interested in her newfound passion for antique roses. Other members of the Rose Rustlers included Margaret Sharpe (vice president), Conrad Tips (vice president for publications), Mitzi VanSant (vice president for membership), and Joe Woodard (executive committee chairman). In November of that year, Pam published the very first edition of *The Old Texas Rose* newsletter. She asked me, as president of the Rose Rustlers, to provide an opening letter for *The Old Texas Rose*. In that letter, I wrote:

> This newsletter is meant to be a vehicle for old rose growers to share their knowledge. Many of us enjoy 'The Rose Letter' published by The Heritage Rose Group. This Texas newsletter is meant to further promote interest in old roses, and to explore their potential as landscape plants for our state. We plan to do this through articles, plant sharing and collecting trips. We hope that you will not only join the organization but lend your active support to its objectives.

In an article in this first issue, Pam recalled that James W. "Buddy" Harrison suggested "Welch's Night Raiders" as the name for our organization, and S. J. Derby proposed "The Ragged, Ragged Robins" (none of us looked too hot on collecting trips, and Ragged Robin was the common name for a particular old rose). As the group's secretary, Pam insisted that "as we were a collection of giant intellects ourselves, we should reflect the scholarly as opposed to the larcenous aspect of our organization in our title." She added, however, "I get the feeling that everyone will end up calling us 'The Texas Rose Rustlers' anyway!" Sure enough, that name stuck, and momentum grew as more and more interested gardeners joined the organization and began their own searches for rose treasures.

As time progressed, various journalists visited the group. In an August 1987 *Horticulture* magazine article titled "On the Trail with Texas Rose Rustlers," garden writer Tom Christopher wrote:

> Admittedly, these Texans' interest in antique roses is hardly unique. In the last few years the so-called old roses—the cultivars bred before the rise of the modern Hybrid Tea—have become the most fashionable of flowers. . . . If the Texans do not stand alone in this interest, though, their

ABOVE: Early Texas Rose Rustlers.

Newsletters of the Texas Rose Rustlers are still valuable today as chronicles of the earliest local discoveries.

expertise and their flamboyant style surely puts them in a class by themselves.

Ink Mendelsohn from the Smithsonian News Service accompanied the Texas Rose Rustlers on a typical foray to several Central Texas towns including Weimar, Schulenburg, and Bellville. She wrote about the experience, giving the group more national coverage. Her exceptional article (*Houston Chronicle Magazine*, July 3, 1988) is pertinent even today. To illustrate the value of rustling roses, Mendelsohn mentioned the event that Pam described as the "first real bonanza," when the group visited Raymond Fisher's garden in Bellville to collect roses inherited from his Austin County forebears. "Two years later," Mendelsohn wrote, "Fisher died, and his garden was bulldozed. But the likes of 'Cramoisi Superieur' and 'Paul's Scarlet' now live on in other gardens."

According to Becky Smith, a longtime active member of the present-day Texas Rose Rustlers, the organization has changed with the years, but it still has the same purpose of joining together to share and gain knowledge. Actual rustles have changed into "cutting exchanges," as the numbers are too large for old-fashioned rustles. Smaller group rustles are encouraged, and rustling etiquette is endorsed on the group's website (www.texasroserustlers.com). The group is as friendly as ever and strives to keep the love of old garden roses and new roses that behave as old garden roses fervently alive. The friendships formed around the common love of these roses last a lifetime.

Old roses were often found in cemeteries, where "time stood still" (image courtesy of Faith Bickley).

RULES OF RUSTLING *Greg Grant*

Of all the plants that inspire rustling, roses top the list. After all, roses are the most popular flower in the world for a reason. Unfortunately, there aren't as many old roses out there as there used to be. Development, disaster, and do-gooders (cleaning up) have doomed many a survivor. That's why it's so important to save as many as we can. With wimpy new roses bred for other parts of the world being introduced all the time, and the Knock Out® roses being planted ad nauseam from sprawl to mall, it's critical that we save the genetic diversity and history of these old proven treasures.

According to Mr. Webster and friends, rustling involves "moving, bringing, or getting by energetic action" or "steal[ing] livestock." To the uninitiated, it may sound like a bit of a rogue activity, with less-than-refined participants running roughshod over the landscape singing "gnome on the range." But it actually involves more of a cultural and horticultural treasure hunt with scholarly overtones. When searching for roses (or any other plant) that got away from the herd, it's very important to be aware of both garden and social ethics. After all, gardeners look best in situ, not in the county jail. So to avoid any troubles, commit this list of rustling commandments to memory.

1. Never trespass on private property. I'm not sure about other states, but in Texas folks will shoot you in the aster!

2. Find the owner and ask permission to propagate the plant. Always offer to exchange money, other plants, or your firstborn if need be.

3. Take only cuttings, never the entire plant. Plants that have survived for years on a site have earned the right to be there. They are a living part of history. They may also mark the location of houses, flower beds, or property lines for future owners or historians, so leave them alone! Only if destruction of a site by a dozer is imminent should a rose (or any plant) be completely removed.

4. Always tidy up the parent plant by removing volunteer woody plants and other weeds growing with it, pruning out the dead wood, fertilizing it, and mulching it if you can. Everybody and everything needs a hand at some point in time.

5. Write down the name of the owner and the location of the plant for future reference. Since knowing its true name is often impossible, give the plant a study name like "Cedar Cemetery Cream" or "Granny's Pink Tea" that can be passed around with it. I like to use names that designate the person or place from which they came.

THE ANTIQUE ROSE EMPORIUM

*I*n the spring of 1983 I attended the old rose symposium at the Huntington Botanical Gardens in Los Angeles. The rose collection there was an eye-opener for me. It was fun to meet others interested in old roses and to identify in real life some of the roses I had only read about previously. I was particularly impressed with 'Marie Pavié' (1888, blush white and fragrant). There was a hedge of them at the Huntington. Since then it has become a favorite for containers, low masses, and almost continuous bloom. As the Rose Rustlers continued to gather mystery roses and become excited about their potential as garden plants, it was obvious that they needed a source for them.

Huntington Botanical Gardens Antique Rose Symposium.

I had met Mike Shoup in 1982 while he was working on a master's degree in horticulture from Texas A&M University. He was operating a native plant nursery in nearby Independence, Texas. Mike was enthusiastic about my suggestion for starting a nursery devoted to old garden roses and growing and developing them from cuttings rather than budding them onto understocks, which was the accepted practice in the existing rose industry. Typical commercial rose growers almost always

Mike Shoup, of the Antique Rose Emporium (ARE).

T-budded hybrid teas onto rootstocks such as 'Dr. Huey' or Rosa multiflora. Those of us interested in old roses were asking, "Why not grow old roses from cuttings as our ancestors did?"

My wife, Diane, suggested the name "Antique Rose Emporium" for our new partnership. Working with the Texas Rose Rustlers and interested rose collectors around the world, the Antique Rose Emporium began to propagate and grow roses to offer by mail order. Ten thousand copies of our first catalog were printed for the 1982–1983 season.

Soon after the inception of the Antique Rose Emporium, we also began to offer companion perennials such as oxeye daisy, native yellow columbines, German red carnations, cemetery white iris, standing phlox, bouncing bet, yarrow, and Brazos penstemon. William Lanier Hunt from Raleigh, North Carolina, a lover of old roses and founding father of the Southern Garden History Society, identified our old "white flags" as *Iris × albicans*, a native of Yemen. They came to us via the Spanish, who had received them from the first Moorish conquerors of Spain. They were even then called "cemetery iris." No wonder they don't mind our Texas heat!

One way we chose to introduce the public to old roses involved Neiman Marcus in Dallas. In my mind the most prestigious commercial catalog at the time was Neiman's Christmas catalog. Mike Shoup and I went to Dallas and proposed offering collections of old garden roses in this catalog. We

An early catalog cover with a Texas country cottage porch scene (image courtesy of Cynthia Mueller).

The 1986-87 Antique Rose Emporium Catalogue

suggested "Republic of Texas," "Fragrance," and "Victorian" collections. This created considerable interest and helped stimulate sales for old garden roses and was repeated for several years in their catalog.

But catalog customers weren't satisfied with ordering plants. They wanted to see larger specimens in garden settings. Washington County was already a destination for many people when Texas bluebonnets bloomed in the spring. Independence was highly important as a historical site, with Sam Houston's wife's home, the oldest continually active Baptist church in Texas, and the remains of old Baylor University. Having a garden where people could visit and purchase plants seemed to be a good idea.

We found and purchased the old Hairston homesite in 1985. Nancy Volkman, ASLA, from the Texas A&M University Landscape Architecture Department, assisted with the landscape plan, and Gordon Echols, an architect also on the Texas A&M faculty, researched the historical details of the structures on the site. The nursery was an exhausting weekend venture for Diane and me, but ultimately all of our efforts resulted in the re-creation of the Hairston Kitchen Garden and the development of a demonstration antique rose and perennial garden. An old barn was converted into a sales

The Hairston
Kitchen garden
at ARE, featuring
roses and many
compatible
perennials.

ARE Hairston
Kitchen Garden
before restoration
and planting.

ARE 'Lamarque'
rose on arch at
Hairston Kitchen.

office and a log corn crib became the gift shop. We opened the garden center in the spring of 1986 with an event that included a string quartet and catered meal.

At this same time, several publishers approached me about writing a book about old garden roses and perennials. Friend Neil Sperry offered to write the foreword, and I realized that something was going to "have to give" in my schedule. After many months of work, the book (*Perennial Garden Color*, Taylor Publishing, 1989) became a reality and was a big help in supporting the concept of perennials and landscape roses for Southern gardens. Nurserymen, garden club members, and other enthusiastic Texas gardeners helped make it a national best seller. County extension horticulturists in Texas provided a great deal of information and support. Texas Garden Clubs established a scholarship for landscape horticulture students in the Horticulture Department at Texas A&M with proceeds from sales of the book.

Eventually, Mike Shoup and I decided that the Antique Rose Emporium could prosper under his sole leadership. He and Jean Shoup along with the capable staff at the Antique Rose Emporium continued to increase the production and quality of the roses. One of the biggest changes compared with other rose nurseries was growing the roses on their own roots and providing them in containers pretty much year round. Large quantities made them obtainable by the landscape industry, where they almost immediately became "available" instead of "rare." The emporium later expanded to include a garden center in Dahlonega, Georgia, and another in San Antonio, Texas. I enjoyed speaking at various occasions at the San Antonio facility and photographed the garden there extensively for my subsequent books *Antique Roses for the South* (Taylor, 1990) and *The Bountiful Flower Garden*, coauthored with Dr. Neil Odenwald (Taylor, 2000). These were followed by *Heirloom Gardening in the South*, coauthored with Greg Grant (Texas A&M University Press, 2012), and *The Bulb Hunter*, coauthored with Chris Wiesinger (Texas A&M University Press, 2013).

The garden centers in Independence, San Antonio, and Dahlonega became important destinations for gardeners from all across the country. The landscape in San Antonio featured hay bale stucco walls and low-water landscapes. Later, the Antique Rose Emporium decided to concentrate on just the one location in Independence and closed the others. This novel enterprise, however, spawned others throughout the country.

Innovative garden accessories at ARE.

King's Nursery.

Jason and Shelley
Powell's Alabama
nursery, Petals
from the Past.

Chamblee's Rose Nursery of Tyler, Texas, has been growing roses since 1953. It features more than two hundred various roses. Tyler has been the rose capital of Texas for several generations, and the Chamblees are enthusiastically carrying on that tradition with wholesale, retail, and mail-order offerings. Another important nursery is King's Nursery in Tenaha, Texas. King's celebrated one hundred years of service in 2015. Roses, fruiting plants, vegetables, and floral products are all part of the King family nursery. Old specimens of 'Climbing Cecile Brunner' and 'Reve d'Or' mark the King's Nursery site, where visitors are welcomed today by the same family pride and hospitality that have distinguished the nursery all these years. The Arbor Gate Nursery in Tomball, Texas, also offers a large selection of antique roses and even carries a "Greg Grant Signature Collection" including a number of his found roses and other plant introductions. And certainly Jason Powell and his Petals from the Past Nursery in Jemison, Alabama, were inspired by our work at the Antique Rose Emporium. These and many other fine nurseries across the country now offer both new and old cultivars of landscape roses along with other tried and true, locally adapted, organic, and low-water-use garden plants. I think the Antique Rose Emporium helped usher in this new "old" gardening trend. Sharing plants and gardening information has always been more than just a business.

BILL'S FAVORITE ROSES

"Maggie"

Maggie Traweek certainly left her mark at her farm in northeastern Louisiana. My late wife, Diane, was her only grandchild and they were very close. She passed away during the summer of 1967 shortly after a mutual friend had introduced Diane and me. Diane was an only child of two only children. Her parents, Norvel and Leo Thames, lived in Baton Rouge but spent considerable time at the farm, some of which had been passed down since before the Civil War. I heard many stories from friends and family in the Mangham, Louisiana, community about Maggie's garden that included lots of bulbs, camellias, azaleas, iris, and assorted flowering shrubs.

Several years after Maggie's death, I noticed that there were old camellias and azaleas as well as many bulbs surviving without care. There were also two roses that appeared interesting. One was given the study name "Maggie." Almost every time I passed by the abandoned home it was in bloom. The flowers were fairly large, bright pink, and highly fragrant. When you rubbed the stem just below the flower and smelled your fingers, they smelled like black pepper.

"Maggie" has been found in a number of locations and so far there is no consensus about its identity. It has proven to be a great performer in Southern gardens. I observed it in Bermuda, and Greg saw it in Belize.

"Maggie" was one of the earliest found roses (image courtesy of Ralph Anderson).

Swamp rose (*Rosa palustris scandens*)

About fifty feet away from the "Maggie" specimen on the Thames farm near Mangham, I noticed a two- to three-foot shrub that looked like a rose, but I hadn't seen any blooms on it. That wasn't too surprising since it was surviving in a grove of small to medium-sized pine trees. I took cuttings along with those from "Maggie" and brought them back to College Station. These bloomed the next spring for several weeks with fragrant, soft pink flowers that nearly covered gracefully arching limbs.

I was puzzled by it and studied various rose catalogs and books trying to get a clue to its identity. I found an inexpensive copy of *Redouté's Les Roses* and was enjoying the beautiful, detailed drawings when I came upon *R. hudsoniana scandens*, the swamp rose. This rose is now known as *R. palustris scandens*, the semiweeping, semi-double-flowering form. It seemed to be a fit. Redouté had painted the rose collection at Malmaison, home of Empress Josephine of France (1763–1814). One of the original editions of Les Roses sold at auction for $8 million. I didn't feel qualified to get into the bidding but did find it exciting to feel sure that my rose was the same one that Redouté painted.

The swamp rose has been highly disease and insect resistant in my garden. I enjoyed for years a specimen near the front entrance of our Langford Street home in College Station. I felt a need to prune it each year after the spring bloom because it becomes quite large. When pruning, it's best to remove a few old canes and shape the plant rather than give it an overall shearing. This approach will leave its beautiful natural structure intact. It is very adaptable in terms of soil and water conditions, thriving in both wet and dry locations. It's

The swamp rose, *Rosa palustris scandens*, was a favorite of Empress Josephine of France (1763–1814) (image courtesy of Ralph Anderson).

BERMUDA MYSTERY ROSES *Greg Grant*

Bermuda is a very small place (only twenty square miles) and is six hundred miles from the nearest landmass. I visited there as a guest of the Bermuda Rose Society and was fascinated by the roses being grown and the link to the past shared by rose collectors such as Liesbeth Cooper. Liesbeth received the 2006 World Rose Award from the World Federation of Rose Societies for her work identifying and preserving old Bermuda roses.

Recently, the Bermuda Rose Society published a new book that combines its experience with its "Old Bermuda Roses" and recent experiments with more modern garden roses and miniatures. *Roses in Bermuda Revisited* (Bermuda Rose Society, 2013) is edited by Lee Davidson and Liesbeth Cooper. This is a great source of information on rose selections for our area and is a joy to read. It is inspirational to realize that Bermuda has acted as a repository for some of the oldest roses and to compare notes regarding these and old Southern favorites from the United States.

Although annual rainfall in Bermuda averages fifty-eight inches, residents have little access to underground water. Instead they rely on rainfall capture for nearly all their water needs. We can certainly learn from their water management practices and experience with regulating water use in the garden as we strive for water conservation in our landscapes.

Some of the favorites in Bermuda that we have in common are 'Agrippina' or 'Cramoisi Superieur,' 'Archduke Charles,' 'Belinda's Dream,' 'Ducher,' "Caldwell Pink," "Smith's Parish," 'Carefree Beauty,' 'Cecile Brunner,' 'Duchesse de Brabant,' Fortuniana, "Maggie," 'Pacific,' the Green Rose, "Highway 290 Pink Buttons," 'Lamarque,' "Martha Gonzales," 'Mutabilis,' 'Old Blush' ("Parson's Pink China"), "McClinton Tea," 'Mrs. B. R. Cant,' 'Mrs. Dudley Cross,' 'Perle d'Or,' 'Prosperity,' 'Queen Elizabeth,' 'Reve d'Or,' yellow and white Lady Banks, 'Sombreuil,' 'Souvenir de la Malmaison,' 'Souvenir de St. Anne's,' 'The Fairy,' and 'Veilchenblau.'

What we call "Maggie" used to be commonly known in Bermuda as the "Cabbage Rose." It is such a distinctive rose that it is always recognized. More information is available in the book *Mystery Roses around the World*, edited by Virginia Kean with an introduction by Stephen Scanniello. It is published by the Heritage Rose Foundation.

thought to be the only rose capable of growing in permanently wet conditions such as at the edge of streams. Iron chlorosis (yellowing of the foliage caused by iron deficiency) can occur in very alkaline soils. This may be treated by adding sulfur or iron products to the soil.

As I reflect on this rose, I remember two locations that were special. Before Hurricane Katrina there was a native plant section at Longue Vue House and Gardens in New Orleans. Lucille and I toured Longue Vue Gardens in the spring of 2014 and were delighted to see that the original swamp rose plant had resprouted and was in full bloom. Another memorable specimen is in the corner of a formal courtyard at Jason and Shelley Powell's Petals from the Past Nursery in Jemison, Alabama, where it is frequently photographed during its long spring bloom period.

'Belinda's Dream' (Basye)

Dr. Robert Basye modestly wrote in a letter to me dated January 25, 1987, "Last summer I budded onto *R. fortuniana* a rose I think you should have . . . a cross I made some twenty years ago. The bush is of Hybrid Tea stature, a very prolific ever-bloomer, and need never be sprayed. I will not describe it further except to say that after twenty years of observation I give it very high marks." Dr. Robert Basye was a math professor

'Belinda's Dream' has become one of the most popular garden roses in the South (image courtesy of Ralph Anderson).

at Texas A&M University until he retired to the country to breed thornless roses with black spot resistance. He worked with roses for more than fifty years before he died in February 2000. Dr. Basye thought 'Belinda's Dream' needed further "improvement" and was going to destroy it, but when I asked him whether it could be shared with the public, he agreed.

The large, double, bright pink flowers attract immediate attention whether on the bush or in a vase, and they are fragrant as well as visually arresting. I have grown 'Belinda's Dream' on *R. fortuniana* rootstock and on its own roots and found it to be slightly more vigorous as a grafted plant, but useful either way. Disease resistance has been very good. It has now been in existence for twenty-seven years and continues to gain popularity across the South. Its vigor, fragrance, beauty, and disease resistance make it a compelling choice as a shrub or prolific source of cut flowers. Like the old roses, it thrives on its own roots, rooting easily from cuttings and quickly maturing into a useful garden plant. I have seen it used effectively as a hedge and as a large, rounded shrub. The many-petaled buds will sometimes ball in humid weather.

In the spring of 2013, Greg Grant told me that he had found a climbing sport of 'Belinda's Dream,' which he named 'Farmer's Dream.' Greg never ceases to amaze me! He has a sharp eye and an exceptional ability to spot unique variation in plants. Most plant people would immediately patent a rose with that potential, but Greg just wants to share it. He gave me four one-gallon plants in the fall of 2013. I planted three on trellises at the Pebble Creek house and one at my wife Lucille's place, which we call Twin Oaks. I fiercely protected the ones at Pebble Creek recently while painters were refinishing the iron trellises. I can hardly wait to see how they are going to turn out! In May 2014 we visited Greg's gardens and 'Farmer's Dream' was in full bloom. Our friend and photographer Ralph Anderson was able to capture their beauty.

"Petite Pink Scotch"

My former professor and friend Richard Stadtherr at Louisiana State University gave me a gallon-sized plant of this rose in 1980. Dr. Stadtherr suggested that I try it as a shrub or ground cover in Texas. He had received his original plant from the National Arboretum, where it had been tested since 1956 and was considered useful as a bank plant. The original specimen had been found in 1949 by Jackson M. Batchelor of Willard, North Carolina, growing in the garden of a 1750s plantation on the Cape Fear River near Wilmington, North Carolina.

The plant is truly distinctive. Although the name given it by the National Arboretum would lead one to believe that it is derived from the Scotch rose (*Rosa spinosissima*), I agree with Charles Walker (at the time president of the Heritage Rose Foundation), who is quite certain that this rose is a hybrid of *R. wichuraiana*. The tiny

"Petite Pink Scotch" rose was discovered growing in the garden of a 1750s plantation on the Cape Fear River near Wilmington, North Carolina (image courtesy of Ralph Anderson).

evergreen leaves form two- to three-foot mounds of cascading branches that are covered with dime-sized, fully double, pale pink flowers for several weeks each spring. The tips of the branches root where they touch the ground, making it a good ground-cover plant. It is a good idea to prune the plants severely every two to three years to keep them neat.

"Petite Pink Scotch" is a very tough plant. It does prefer neutral to slightly acidic soil. For the first several years I grew it, there were no insect or disease problems at all, but spider mites later found my plants irresistible. "Petite Pink Scotch" is an unusual rose that can be useful on modest slopes. One of the nicest plantings of it I have seen is on the banks of a water garden at Petals from the Past Nursery near Jemison, Alabama.

"Natchitoches Noisette"

It is gratifying to see how popular "Natchitoches Noisette" has become. Public plantings of it in New Orleans and other cities attest to its usefulness as a four- to six-foot-tall, nearly ever-blooming shrub.

I don't know for certain that this rose is a Noisette; later research indicates that it is probably a China. I found it marking a gravesite in the old American Cemetery in Natchitoches, Louisiana. The rather small (1½–2 inch), semidouble flowers are light pink and China-like, with darker pink reverses on the petals. They bloom in medium-sized clusters and have a light Noisette fragrance. The plant from which I took cuttings was in bloom

"Natchitoches Noisette" was discovered by Bill Welch in the old American Cemetery in Natchitoches, Louisiana (image courtesy of Ralph Anderson).

at Christmas and tends to be in flower much of the year. Hodges Gardens near Many, Louisiana, has a rooted cutting from the original planted among the China roses. "Natchitoches Noisette" is a little like 'Champneys' Pink Cluster' but with much better disease resistance and somewhat less intense fragrance. It roots easily and responds well to pruning.

I have enjoyed using "Natchitoches Noisette" as a specimen near the front entrance at our home in

Louisiana. Because it repeat flowers frequently it combines with 'Formosa' (fuchsia) azaleas, Phlox pilosa (lavender pink), yellow and orange daylilies, and heirloom *Narcissus* in shades of yellow and white. Dogwood trees with their layers of white spring flowers frame the picture. The original dogwoods were from Emory Smith of Baton Rouge and have reseeded over the entire garden. For many years a huge specimen of banana shrub (*Michelia figo*) scented the entire area.

Wayne and Cheryl Stromeyer have restored a beautiful home on Highland Road in Baton Rouge, Louisiana. They opened their home and garden to the attendees of the 2011 Southern Garden History Society annual meeting. Highland Road is a beautiful area south of the LSU campus. It roughly parallels the Mississippi River. There are now more than fifty old roses included in the garden. The parterre was started in 1993, the year they moved in, and they completed the installation that same year. The formal camellia garden and the kitchen were installed in 2013.

There is some information about the pattern of the garden in *The New Louisiana Gardener* (Sally Reeves, LSU Press, 2001). The original parterre patterns were laid out by Louis de Feriet in New Orleans sometime between 1820 and 1840. The patterns are illustrated in the New Orleans Notarial Archives in the tenth in a series of color images in the book (plan book 21m, folio 31). The Stromeyers slightly modified the dimensions from the archives drawing. Cheryl had some concerns about a large parterre in the front. She consulted Suzanne Turner, principal of Suzanne Turner Associates, a research and design firm that specializes in historical landscapes. Suzanne provided assurance that the current size was about right.

The garden features "Natchitoches Noisette" roses at strategic places within the parterre. There are also two arches along the sides of the garden that are covered in 'Climbing Old Blush.' In addition to the parterre, the Stromeyers have a beautiful vegetable garden, extensive naturalized heirloom bulbs, and a growing collection of camellias. There is also a nice specimen of 'Marechal Niel' framing the rear entrance of the home.

Russell's cottage rose (*Russelliana*), about 1837

Among the first roses I planted at Rehburg was a gift from native plant authority and friend Lynn Lowrey. Lynn said that he found it growing along a railroad track. Joyce Demitts of Heritage Roses in California identified it for me. While visiting the Huntington Botanical Gardens, I described my "mys-

Russell's Cottage Rose (image courtesy of Mike Shoup).

tery rose" to Joyce and she asked whether I had noticed the pine scent of the new foliage. When I said that I had, she took me to a labeled specimen in full bloom and said, "I think this is your rose?" It's exciting to identify a rose you have been growing and wondering about for several years. A couple of years later, I presented a program on old roses at the University of Texas's Winedale Center near Round Top, and Mrs. Parks, a lady I had known for many years, brought a rose blossom to me for identification. She had wondered about it for years, and tears came to her eyes when I confidently told her that it was Russell's cottage rose.

This rose is occasionally found at old sites in Texas and the Gulf South. Although a spring-only bloomer, it is very tough and disease resistant. The medium-sized double flowers occur in midspring and are a rich purple, changing to lilac as they age. The fragrance is intense and damask-like. It is a useful background or specimen plant. The pine-like scent of the new leaves is unique.

"McClinton Tea"

I discovered this rose in the cottage garden of Mrs. McClinton in an African American neighborhood in Natchitoches, Louisiana, during the Christmas season of 1982. We were visiting Diane's maternal grandmother, who lived

"McClinton Tea" is a bright pink, heavily scented large shrub rose.

just several blocks away. That same day I had found "Natchitoches Noisette" in the old American Cemetery, also in Natchitoches. Some consider Natchitoches to be the oldest community in the Louisiana Purchase. "McClinton Tea" ranks among the very best roses that I grow. Flowers are bright pink, semidouble, and very heavily scented with what I consider typical tea fragrance. The reverse of the petals is much darker than the inside. Like most teas, the plant can be slow to become established but soon becomes a large and beautiful specimen that has excellent disease resistance. Mrs. McClinton was a statuesque lady who graciously welcomed me to her garden after I knocked on her door.

She had numerous specimens planted in a random manner and was pleased to offer me some cuttings. I wish that I had asked Mrs. McClinton how and where she had obtained her plants.

'Old Blush' (1751), 'Climbing Old Blush'

The class of roses we call Chinas originated in that country many years ago. A thousand years before the birth of Christ, the Chinese had bred their single-flowering native roses into true garden types. The revolutionary characteristic

'Old Blush' rose is almost continuously in flower. The masses of strongly pink blooms are very noticeable in the landscape (image courtesy of Ralph Anderson).

of these roses was that they were ever blooming. The ever-blooming quality of all modern roses can be traced back to these early Chinas.

Individual blossoms of most Chinas are not spectacular. These roses are not likely to win "Best of Show," but their profusion of flowers, disease resistance, and typically long, healthy life more than compensate. It is not unusual to find specimens of China roses a hundred years old or older, surviving entirely without human care in Texas and the South. Bloom is heaviest in midspring with sprinklings of flowers all summer. Another heavy bloom in fall usually follows the first good rain showers in September or October.

Chinas are useful as hedges, specimen plants, or borders. If pruned severely, most of them can be easily maintained as small, rounded plants. They respond well to heavy pruning in late winter but seem to resent it in summer. When allowed to grow with only dead or weak wood removed, they slowly attain large size.

'Old Blush' sometimes goes by other names such as "Parson's Pink China," "Old Pink Daily," "Common Monthly," and "Daisy Rose." It is one of the most common, yet pleasant, of the old roses. It bears medium, semidouble, light pink blossoms in many-flowered clusters, which often blush dark rose on the outer edge of the petals in strong sun. 'Old Blush' is constantly in flower, with a really heavy flush in spring. The bush is upright in habit and may bloom eleven months of the year in the Gulf South. When at its peak in spring, 'Old Blush' can rival an azalea in full bloom. Flower quality becomes poor during the heat of summer but improves radically with the first cool days of fall.

Greg's and my friend, the late Cleo Barnwell of Shreveport, Louisiana, introduced me to the climbing form of 'Old Blush.' Cleo was a friend of Elizabeth Lawrence (1904–1985), the famous garden writer from Charlotte, North Carolina. Miss Lawrence shared a cutting of 'Climbing Old Blush' with her and it thrived in Cleo's garden. I presented a program in Charlotte at Wing Haven Gardens, which is on Ridgewood Avenue near the Lawrence garden. I was able to visit Miss Lawrence's garden, which was then owned by Mrs. Mary Lindeman Wilson. I saw the original plant that provided the cuttings for Cleo Barnwell. While visiting with Mrs. Wilson, I learned that Miss Lawrence had obtained her cutting from Elizabeth Clarkson, owner of Wing Haven, a neighbor on Ridgewood Avenue. Upon further questioning of docents at Wing Haven, I learned that Mrs. Clarkson had brought her 'Climbing Old Blush' with her from Uvalde, Texas, when she moved to Charlotte in 1922. Lindy Wilson has transferred ownership of Miss Lawrence's house and garden to the Garden Conservancy, and exciting restoration work is in progress. Lindy has graciously shared other Elizabeth Lawrence plants with me such as her 'White Empress' camellia and white Lady Banks rose. She also shared several of Miss Lawrence's rain lilies when I visited her "new" Charlotte garden in October 2014. Lindy's new garden is delightful. It includes many plants from the Lawrence garden and other perennials, bulbs, and ornamentals.

'Climbing Old Blush' is a vigorous climber. After I shared my cuttings with the Antique Rose Emporium, it was planted on many sites including the front trellises at the Admiral Nimitz Museum in Fredericksburg, Texas.

"Caldwell Pink"

Caldwell, Texas, is a small town about twenty-five miles west of College Station on Highway 21, which is my route when going to Austin, San Antonio, or South Texas. In 1980 I noticed a small nursery and greenhouse and stopped to check it out. The owner, Mrs. Webb, had several three- to five-foot-tall rose bushes growing in her garden. When I inquired about them she indicated that they bloomed often and in abundance. I asked about cuttings and she was pleased to share them. I wish now that I had asked more about their

"Caldwell Pink" is a low-growing rose with masses of small, very double pink flowers. It is suitable for hedges or specimens in the flower bed (images courtesy of Mike Shoup).

past. Within a year the nursery closed and I was told that Mrs. Webb had passed away.

I decided to put the study name "Caldwell Pink" on the rose. It proved to be a really tough, drought- and disease-resistant rose. Small, very double pink flowers cover the plant much of the year. The only negative thing about it is its lack of strong fragrance. I find it useful as a three- to five-foot hedge or specimen plant.

'Souvenir de la Malmaison' (Beluze, 1843)

Malmaison was Empress Josephine's country estate outside Paris. This rose did not grow there amid her fine collection but was introduced after her death and named in honor of her garden. Many collectors of old roses consider it to be the finest Bourbon rose ever created. It is the most reliably repeat-flowering Bourbon I have grown and the only one I have found surviving in old Southern gardens. Thomas Affleck, the great nurseryman and writer, said of 'Souvenir de la Malmaison' in 1856, "How I envy the grower who first saw that plant in bloom, the seed of which he had sown, feeling that such a gem was his!"

Pam Puryear first found this rose in Anderson, Texas, at the home of Mary Minor. After researching the find for many months, we finally agreed that we had found the famous 'Souvenir de la Malmaison.' In 1983, while searching for roses in Brenham, we discovered at the home of Mrs. Carl Meyer what appeared to be a very similar rose except that it was pure white.

'Souvenir de la Malmaison' is considered by many rose collectors to be the finest Bourbon rose ever created (image courtesy of Ralph Anderson).

This rose was later identified as 'Kronprinzessin Viktoria,' the white sport of 'Souvenir' that was released in 1888. It is even more compact than the mannerly 'Souvenir' and rarely exceeds two to three feet. The climbing sport of 'Souvenir de la Malmaison' was introduced in 1893 and appears to have the good qualities of the bush type in the climbing form.

We questioned the identity of Mary Minor's rose because her plant was at least six feet tall and wide. Our references listed its size as three to four feet. When questioned about its origin and her growing practices, Mary Minor indicated she had received it from a lady she worked for and she had put lots of "improvement" in the soil. She further defined "improvement" as rotten cow manure. I remember seeing only one other 'Souvenir' that I believe was really old. It was at a large farmhouse north of Schulenburg, Texas. The combination of a nice shrub form and exquisite, fragrant flowers is hard to beat. Black spot occurred on all the ones I have grown. However, when a sunny site with good air circulation is chosen, black spot does not severely limit the pleasure of growing this magnificent rose.

I have enjoyed learning about 'Souvenir de St Anne's' (before 1916), introduced by Hiling in 1950. A beautiful specimen in the garden of Richard and Barbara Powell near Independence, Texas, is vigorous and free flowering. It is considered to be a sport of 'Souvenir de la Malmaison,' but the blooms have fewer petals and the plant appears to be somewhat larger and a bit more vigorous. 'Souvenir de St Anne's' seems to bloom more and provide more landscape color than its parent (which is saying a lot).

"Peggy Martin" (air conditioner rose)

Peggy Martin has been a mainstay in the New Orleans Old Garden Rose Society for many years. She and her husband, MJ, lived in Plaquemines Parish a few miles across the Mississippi River from New Orleans. My wife, Diane, and I were their guests several years ago when I accepted a speaking engagement for the New Orleans Old Garden Rose Society.

Peggy graciously cared for us during our visit and entertained us in her home with a memorable Louisiana-style seafood boil that had been harvested by her husband just hours before. Peggy's garden included a wonderful collection of several hundred old roses assembled with love and care over the years. There were many specimens that appealed to me, but one rambler in particular caught my eye. I am always interested in thornless roses, and Peggy was particularly enthusiastic about a large, healthy specimen she had collected in 1989 in New Orleans. According to Peggy, "I was given cuttings of the thornless climber in 1989 by Ellen Dupriest, who had gotten it from a relative's garden in New Orleans. When I first saw this rose it was in full bloom and smothered the 8 ft wooden fence in Ellen's back yard. It took my breath away! I had never seen a rose so lushly beautiful with thornless, bright green foliage that was disease free. All along the canes there were clusters of roses that resembled perfect nosegays of blooms."

"Peggy Martin." This showy, thornless climbing rose was collected in 1989 by Peggy Martin in New Orleans (image courtesy of Ralph Anderson).

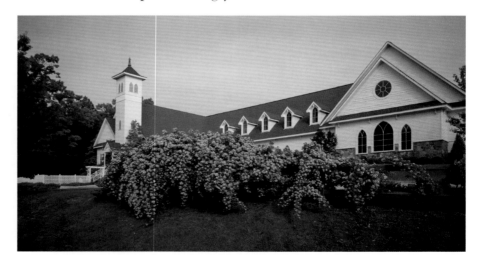

I departed from New Orleans in the late summer of 2003 with several cuttings of Peggy's thornless climber. I was pleased that the cuttings rooted quickly and I immediately set one on the fence that encloses the air conditioner equipment at Fragilee, which was then our weekend place in Washington County, Texas. We called it the "Air Conditioner Rose." I was a little dubious of the site I had selected because the soil was less than ideal. My concern soon disappeared as I saw the cutting quickly mature into a vigorous specimen that spans most of the twelve to fifteen linear feet of four-foot-tall picket fencing.

I didn't allow myself to get overexcited about the plant because I assumed that it would be a "once bloomer" with a fairly short flowering season in the spring. On a subsequent visit with Peggy, she indicated that my plant would rebloom in the fall once it had been established for a couple of years. I must admit that I had some doubt about the rebloom in our hot and sometimes very dry Texas climate. The next year Peggy's rose rewarded us with a modest but welcome bloom from September through November. Even after it was covered by ice for two days during mid-December 2005, we had some scattered bloom all winter.

We fretted about many of our New Orleans friends during Hurricane Katrina on August 29, 2005. Getting information was not easy with so much of the communications system inoperative. We were also uneasy about traveling to Birmingham for an annual meeting with the gardens staff for *Southern Living* magazine. We spent the night of September 7 at our home in Mangham, Louisiana. Mangham is in the northeastern part of the state, and Katrina had only brushed by as it veered to the east through Mississippi. We were relieved that our cotton and soybean crops received only minor damage and the old pecan trees in our yard suffered little more than loss of most of the current year's crop.

Upon arrival in Birmingham, we checked into the Marriott Courtyard near the *Southern Living* headquarters and were seated adjacent to two couples with New Orleans accents. After introducing ourselves, we learned that they were from Plaquemines Parish and had lost their homes. Birmingham was the first place they had been able to find shelter. I asked them whether they knew Peggy Martin and her family. They replied that they knew them well and asked whether we knew about their tragic losses. Peggy had lost both her elderly parents in the flood that inundated nearly all of Plaquemines Parish. We were, of course, deeply saddened that Peggy had lost her parents, her home, and the commercial fishing boat that her husband had used to

Peggy Martin, longtime rose collector, found that her namesake rose was the only survivor in her garden after Hurricane Katrina (image courtesy of Ralph Anderson).

supplement their income.

It took a couple of months for me to reestablish communication with Peggy. She and her family had moved to Gonzales, Louisiana, which is close to Baton Rouge on Interstate 10. I asked Peggy about her roses and home in Plaquemines Parish. She told me that the house and garden were under about twenty feet of saltwater for two weeks following the hurricane. When she was finally able to return to visit their property, she was heartened to see the lush growth of her thornless climber, a testament to its toughness and status as a true survivor. This rose and one crinum (milk and wine lily) were all that remained of the once-beautiful garden.

I was already convinced that this rose deserved to be made widely available and enjoyed by gardeners in other locations. Its disease resistance, thornless stems, and colorful displays of bright pink flowers along with a graceful vining form make it a logical choice for creating beautiful garden pictures. My specimen is literally covered with clusters of pink flowers each spring from mid-March through May. It starts to bloom again in late summer and repeats until a hard frost slows it down for the winter.

An idea came to me in the middle of the night about growing "Peggy Martin" as a fund-raiser for the Zone IX Horticulture Restoration Fund that had been established by the Garden Club of America. Nancy Godshall with the Garden Club of Houston was enthusiastic about the project as well and provided valued guidance. The purpose would be to help restore parks, gardens, and green space in New Orleans, Louisiana; Laurel, Mississippi; and Beaumont, Texas, following Hurricanes Katrina and Rita.

We were pleased that Mike and Jean Shoup, owners of the Antique Rose

Emporium; Jason and Shelley Powell, owners of Petals from the Past Nursery in Jemison, Alabama; Mark Chamblee, owner of Chamblee Rose Nursery in Tyler, Texas; Sue Ripley, owner of Naconiche Nursery near Nacogdoches, Texas; Aubrey King, owner of King's Nursery in Tenaha, Texas; and Heidi Sheesley, owner of Treesearch Farms in Houston, Texas, all agreed to donate one dollar to the Garden Restoration Fund for each plant produced and sold.

This became a fun and worthwhile project—a great rose and a great cause. I am fully convinced that the resilience and fortitude of our friends and neighbors in New Orleans, Beaumont, and Mississippi are matched by the beauty and toughness of the "Peggy Martin" rose. This rose is a fitting symbol of survival on the Gulf Coast.

'Perle d'Or' (Rambaux, 1875)

This rose is very similar to 'Cecile Brunner,' the sweetheart rose, but it is a peachy-pink color. Although it is usually compact in form, I have seen six-foot-tall and round specimens. The flowers are very fragrant, and I have seen the plant doing especially well in West Texas. The buds are beautifully formed and relatively small. The plant is effective in masses, in hedges, or as a specimen. Plants are disease resistant and can be spectacular. It is classified as a polyantha.

'Perle d'Or' rose is a polyantha with peachy-pink, beautifully shaped small blooms and buds (image courtesy of Ralph Anderson).

'Mlle. Cecile Brunner,' sweetheart rose (Ducher, 1880), 'Climbing Cecile Brunner' (1894)

This is one of the most widely planted and beloved roses of all time. It was created in France by Joseph Pernet Ducher, who crossed 'Mignonette' and a tea rose named 'Madame de Tartas' to achieve this beautifully formed, lightly fragrant pink masterpiece. Although often referred to by the masculine name Cecil, it was named for a woman called Cecile.

'Climbing Cecile Brunner' was introduced in 1894 and is much more vigorous than the bush form. 'Climbing Cecile Brunner' can reach fifteen to twenty feet on a trellis, fence, or wall. It can also grow in an umbrella form without support. Most of the old plants found in cemeteries are the climbing form. The climber blooms more in spring and fall and rarely in summer.

'Mlle. Cecile Brunner,' the sweetheart rose, is an all-time favorite small-flowered pink polyantha (image courtesy of Ralph Anderson).

'Cecile Brunner' is perfect as a boutonniere rose. Foliage is healthy and usually disease-free. It is classified as a polyantha.

'Ducher' (image courtesy of Mike Shoup).

'Ducher' (Ducher, 1869)

'Ducher' is the only white China rose that I know of. Blooms are very double, flat when open, and pure white. Growth is vigorous but fairly compact. It makes one of the best container roses and blooms continuously. I recall finding this only once on a rose rustle, and that was at an old home in New Braunfels in the mid-1980s. Pam Puryear, Margaret Sharpe, and I came upon it simultaneously. It is a really useful and beautiful plant, but I have lost it during severe cold spells. Perhaps that is why we don't often encounter it in cemeteries or old homesites.

'Prosperity' (Pemberton, 1819)

I first encountered this rose in a small cottage garden owned by a friend of my grandmother, Pearl Orman, in Yoakum, Texas. I gave it the study name "Pearl Orman" at first. It is classified as a hybrid musk and has creamy white buds flushed with pale pink. Small to moderate roses occur in large clusters throughout the growing season. The original plant was set at the corner post of a small porch. I use it today in our front courtyard in College Station on an iron trellis. It is thorny, but it can make a spectacular show in spring with many subsequent blooms throughout the warm season.

'Prosperity' is a Pemberton-bred musk rose that is excellent for draping trellises and arbors.

'Marie Pavié' (Allegatiere, 1888)

My first encounter with 'Marie Pavié' occurred at the Huntington Botanical Gardens, where I saw a low hedge of them in full bloom. The fragrance,

'Marie Pavié' is an excellent container rose for Texas conditions. Semidouble flowers open in clusters and are intensely fragrant.

'Marie Daly' is a darker-colored sport of 'Marie Pavié' discovered by Greg Grant in his garden (image courtesy of Ralph Anderson).

frequency of bloom, and scarcity of thorns, along with the rich green foliage and shapely buds, make this rose one of the best. My initial impression was so strong that I chose to carry a one-gallon plant in my hand luggage on the return trip to Texas from the Huntington Symposium. I have found this to be one of the best container roses. It survives as a container plant in our hot Texas conditions. The only plant I have seen surviving in an old site was in the College Station garden of one of Mattie Rosprim's friends. Cynthia Mueller remembers it in La Grange, Texas, thriving at the edge of the railroad tracks and a sidewalk. It shared the front yard with a beautiful specimen of winter honeysuckle (Lonicera fragrantissima) and shrimp plant (Justicia brande-geeana).

The pale pink buds occur in medium-sized clusters and open to semi-double blush-white flowers. These are intensely fragrant with a wonderful musk scent. Stems are usually thornless, with small prickles occurring on the undersides of the foliage midribs. 'Marie Daly' first appeared as a sport in Greg Grant's garden in the late 1990s. It is much pinker than 'Marie Pavié' but is otherwise identical. The darker pink flowers make it a useful addition.

'La Marne' (Barbier, 1915)

'La Marne' is an excellent landscape rose often used as a hedge. It has ten-petaled flowers with pink edges and creamy white centers occurring in clusters. We have found it in numerous old cemeteries. The fragrant flowers are at their best during the cooler parts of the blooming season.

Bill Welch, Greg Grant, and Jason Powell admire the 'La Marne' rose, often used as a hedge and a true survivor in neglected situations. The flowers are in clusters and have ten petals each, with creamy white centers edged in pink (image courtesy of Ralph Anderson).

Although it sometimes struggles with black spot, it can look good for much of the year. 'La Marne' is one of the most often found old roses in neglected situations and it makes a nice display when massed in the garden.

'Mrs. Dudley Cross' (Paul, 1908)

'Mrs. Dudley Cross' is among the most frequently found and popular of the old garden roses. Study names first suggested by the Rose Rustlers for 'Mrs. Dudley Cross' included the "Hole Rose" and "November Surprise." The full, pale yellow flowers are usually tinged pink. The foliage is exceptionally healthy and disease resistant. It is in the tea rose class, usually thornless, and exceptionally well suited to Southern climates. Teas are the roses that were most popular during the plantation era of the South. They are not only noted for their abundant spring and summer flowers, but are also particularly nice in fall and early winter. They usually assume an upright habit and have bronzy red new foliage.

'Mrs. Dudley Cross.'

Shrub roses 'Mrs. Dudley Cross' and "Natchitoches Noisette" combine well in this historical setting (image courtesy of Ralph Anderson).

'Mrs. Dudley Cross' has good resistance to black spot and likes hot climates. The branches often bow gracefully with the weight of the large blooms. This was considered an elegant trait during Victorian times and is still appreciated by those who enjoy the many distinctive and easily grown roses of the tea class. Fragrance is distinctive and cool, somewhat reminiscent of dried tea leaves.

"Katy Road Pink" ('Carefree Beauty,' Buck, 1979)

This fabulous rose was grown for many years as "Katy Road Pink." It is among the very best roses I have grown. Its vigor, disease resistance, and nearly ever-

"Katy Road Pink" was a found rose for several years before it was discovered to be 'Carefree Beauty.' It is one of the best for Southern gardens, and its fragrant, rose-pink flowers are almost continually present.

blooming qualities make it indispensable as a landscape shrub. It was originally collected along Katy Road in Houston and much later discovered to be 'Carefree Beauty.' It is also highly fragrant and sets large, round hips that turn bright orange at maturity and are useful for decorative purposes. Mature size is four to six feet tall and wide. If maturing flowers are removed, even more blooms will appear. Substance of the petals is good and the buds are beautiful. Each flower has fifteen to twenty petals. I like to use "Katy Road Pink" as a shrub mass in combination with *Salvia farinacea* 'Henry Duelberg.' The rich pink of the roses contrasts nicely with the dark blue spikes of the salvia. Lucille and I have used "Katy Road Pink" in the front garden of our guest house in Independence, Texas.

'Archduke Charles' (Laffay, before 1837)

'Archduke Charles' is described by Ethelyn Emery Keays in her book *Old Roses*. She writes, "The full, lasting flower with outer petals of deep rose red opens in a cupped shape, enclosing in the cup smaller petals of whitish pink to real white . . . the rose color gradually creeps in and over the pale center so entirely that the flower becomes a rose colored bloom." She adds that it is "a fine old rose, much admired in the past."

'Archduke Charles' has a more refined flower than most Chinas. A single bush may appear to bear blooms of several different colors simultaneously because the flowers change rapidly as they age. I have found many 'Archduke Charles' plants in old gardens, especially in South Texas. A large specimen was found in San Marcos, Texas, at the Delqueto residence; it reached the eight-foot eave of the front of the house.

Greg chose to put a hedge of 'Arch-

'Archduke Charles' is suitable for use in plantings typical of the Republic of Texas period of our history (1836–1845). Its blooms will change from deep rose to almost white as the flower ages (image courtesy of Ralph Anderson).

duke Charles' across the length of the porch at the Hairston Kitchen Garden at the Antique Rose Emporium in Independence, Texas. We decided to create that garden solely with plants that were available during the Republic of Texas period of our history (1836–1845). Perennials include cemetery white iris (*Iris × albicans*), Brazos penstemon (*Penstemon tenuis*), oxeye daisies (*Chrysanthemum leucanthemum*), and *Salvia farinacea*.

'Cramoisi Superieur' (and climber) (Coquereau, 1832)

The red China roses were commonly planted throughout the South and are frequently found in cemeteries and old homesites. 'Agrippina,' 'Louis Philippe,' and several other red China roses are similar and frequently confused. This special and important rose is velvety rich crimson with a silvery reverse in a double, cupped form, and it is almost ever blooming.

Dean S. Reynolds Hole, the English rosarian and cleric who is credited with the formation of the Royal National Rose Society, summed up his praise for the China roses in his book *Our Gardens*, published in 1899. "There is no other claimant of the title of *semper florens*, bestowed by an ecumenical council of botanists upon the China or monthly roses— '*Semper, ubique, ab omnibus*'—always, everywhere, for all."

Climbing forms are occasionally found. While in Williamsburg, Virginia,

'Cramoisi Superieur' is the old-fashioned red China most often encountered in Southern gardens. It is very heat tolerant and easy to grow from cuttings. The double flowers are velvety rich crimson with a silvery reverse, and almost ever blooming.

assisting with a garden symposium, Peggy Cornett (from Monticello) and I were looking around some of the older gardens. We discovered a large specimen of an ever-blooming climbing red China rose that caught our attention. We were able to contact the owner, who explained that his aunt had planted the rose in 1890. The house was actually built about that time, which meant it was not "of the period" for Williamsburg. I successfully rooted cuttings and gave some to the Antique Rose Emporium. In 2003 I planted one on the rear gate entrance at Fragilee. It has continued to prosper there.

"Martha Gonzales"

This dwarf red China rose was found by Pam Puryear in Navasota, Texas. It is an engaging and useful single-flowering, ever-blooming compact rose. Its usefulness as an eighteen- to twenty-four-inch hedge and its continuous blooming have endeared it to many as a landscape plant and source of color in the garden. Greg found a vigorous climbing sport of it in San Antonio and introduced it as 'Speedy Gonzales.'

"Martha Gonzales" is a dwarf red China rose that has become very popular as a bright spot of color in the garden. It is in almost continual bloom (image courtesy of Ralph Anderson).

'Marechal Niel' (Pradel, 1864)

'Marechal Niel' is among the most legendary of all roses because of its buttery yellow, full, quartered flowers, vigor, and distinctive fragrance. The light green "lettucy"

'Marechal Niel' is one of the most legendary of the old-fashioned roses because of its buttery yellow full quartered flowers and ability to clothe arbors and trellises well.

foliage is also distinctive, as is its ability to span great distances as a climber. Usually grown outdoors in the South, it is especially cold sensitive when getting started. Perhaps it has degenerated or acquired a virus over the years. Until a vigorous source of propagation material can be verified, 'Marechal Niel' will probably have to remain only in the memory of those of us who have seen and experienced its vigor and fragrance.

Greg and I spent quite a bit of time and effort seeking a healthy source of 'Marechal Niel.' This took us to an old neighborhood in Bryan, where we knocked on Helen Fredel's door to ask about a rose blooming in her side yard. She graciously gave us a tour of her garden and we enjoyed seeing her beautiful and distinctive orange-flowering crossvine (*Bignonia capreolata*). She also pointed out and shared bulbs of her Chinese ground orchids (*Bletilla striata*). I had never seen this plant before and have since found it in numerous places. Mrs. Fredel mentioned that her neighbor Mrs. Opersteny had a nice specimen of 'Marechal Niel.'

Mrs. Opersteny responded to our knock on her door and accepted my offer to pay a modest amount for cuttings of her rose. Her largest plant was trained on her garage wall and it was a nice specimen. Greg rooted the cuttings and shared them with the Antique Rose Emporium, but they were never able to produce a large volume of healthy plants to sell.

I visited with my friend Dr. Robert Basye about our experiences with 'Marechal Niel,' and he said that it would probably thrive if grafted onto *Rosa × fortuniana*. He provided a nice started plant for me the next year, and the last time I visited Cricket Court (a home and garden we owned for seven years near Winedale), it had survived about twenty years.

"Highway 290 Pink Buttons"

Tommy Adams was the first propagator at the Antique Rose Emporium and was fond of this rose. I included it in the landscape in a circular bed in front of the sales office of the garden center. Tiny foliage and nickel-sized, very double pink blooms cover the plant when it is in flower. Its delicacy and charm make it useful as a container plant as well.

With occasional pruning, plants can be kept twelve to eighteen inches tall, but larger specimens are common. Although tolerant of drought and heat to some degree, "Highway 290 Pink Buttons" is known to quickly abort its buds when under stress from high heat and lack of water.

"Highway 290 Pink Buttons" is a small-leaved, low-growing plant with nickel-sized, very double pink flowers. It does well in large containers and is compact enough to mingle with other smaller perennials at the front of the flower bed.

The green rose.

The green rose (*Rosa chinensis viridiflora*, Bambridge and Harrison, prior to 1845)

Rosarians may argue whether or not this flower is beautiful, but all agree that the green rose is different. British rose authority Jack Harkness describes it as an "engaging monstrosity." The green flowers often become bronzy colored in the fall. Flower arrangers find the "flowers" useful and long-lasting subjects. It is found in many gardens of the South and is easily grown.

In early spring 1995 we were visiting Florence and Bill Griffin, longtime friends in the Southern Garden History Society, in Atlanta. Florence and I were fascinated with Roman hyacinths, and while traveling through a small town outside Atlanta, we spotted a circular planting of rare pink Roman hyacinths in full bloom. The owner continued to visit with Bill Griffin and my wife, Diane, while Florence and I helped ourselves (sparingly) to the hyacinths. When we finished, the lady asked us if we would mind digging out an old rose nearby. I agreed to do that. It was a nice-sized specimen of the green rose, which we took back home to Texas with us and enjoyed for many years at Cricket Court.

Two specimens of R. chinensis 'Mutabilis' flank arches in this rather formal landscape (image courtesy of Ralph Anderson).

The butterfly rose (*Rosa chinensis* 'Mutabilis,' prior to 1894)

The butterfly rose is of unknown origin. It grows to about six to seven feet tall and has bronzy new foliage. Single flowers open buff yellow, changing to pink and finally crimson, with all three colors frequently blooming in unison. Like most other China roses, it needs room to grow and blooms ten to eleven months of the year.

The butterfly rose is great to use as a single specimen or a hedge. Shaping rather than major pruning works best. Powdery mildew sometimes occurs in spring but usually disappears with the heat of summer. I have never found it occurring in an old garden, but I consider it one of the most useful landscape plants of all the old roses I have experience with.

In 2003, a group of us attended the Chelsea Flower Show and also enjoyed a visit to the Chelsea Physic Garden. Along a path close to the front gate, a shrub of *R. chinensis* 'Sanguinea,' also known as red Bengal rose, takes pride of place. The blooms resemble those of 'Mutabilis' but are a deep scarlet red and a bit larger. We arranged with the garden staff to receive some cuttings and have enjoyed growing them. For a number of years we had two fine specimens on display at the Horticulture Garden at Texas A&M University and also had it at our home in Mangham, Louisiana. We understand that it is still available at the Chelsea Physic Garden and nurseries such as Greenmantle Nursery in California. SFA Gardens in Nacogdoches, Texas, still has a large specimen that I shared with them, as well. This is a large, vigorous-growing China with unusually large flowers and should probably be used more for hedges and specimens.

'Zephirine Drouhin' (Bizot, 1868)

'Zephirine Drouhin' is a distinctive rose for several reasons. The three-inch flowers are cerise pink with a white base, have twenty-five to thirty petals, occur mostly in spring, and have an intense damask fragrance. Foliage is light, soft, and vigorous, with pliant thornless stems. The plant lends itself well to being trained on a trellis or fence.

Because of its thornless nature it is easy to handle and maintain. One of the most beautiful specimens I have seen is at the British Embassy garden in Washington, DC, where the vines are trained on a brick wall surrounding beautiful windows. Fall blooming usually occurs after the second year. I set out four 'Zephirine Drouhin' plants at Twin Oaks and they quickly covered two arches and bloomed nicely in the spring. The thornless stems make training the plants a joy. We look forward to the spring blooming season each year.

'Zepherine Drouhin' at the British Embassy, Washington, DC.

Lady Banks (*Rosa banksiae* 'Lutea,' 1824)

Lady Banks rose was discovered in China in 1807 and named for the wife of the Royal Horticultural Society president, Lord Banks. The flowers are double, about an inch in diameter, and appear for three to four weeks in spring. The graceful arching habit of the thornless canes along with its vigor and drought tolerance places Lady Banks among the most useful of old roses.

The white *Rosa banksiae* 'Alba Plena' was discovered in China in 1807 and imported to England. It does have some thorns, but also a

Lady Banks rose is found in both yellow and white forms and can grow into a huge canopy of narrow, healthy foliage covered with clusters of small flowers for a lengthy period in the spring (image courtesy of Ralph Anderson).

delightful violet scent. Banks roses rarely have pests or diseases. Their greatest enemy is severe cold. While visiting Lindy Wilson, who owned the home of Elizabeth Lawrence in Charlotte, North Carolina, for many years, I was given cuttings of the white Lady Banks rose and brought them back to Texas. Cynthia Mueller was able to root them and we planted one on the gazebo at Fragilee. We watched in awe as it quickly covered the entire structure. It makes an impressive display each year when it blooms. As the plant matures the bark begins flaking off and reveals cinnamon-colored, shaggy wood.

Whether white or yellow, Lady Banks roses tend to make a very impressive display of foliage and flowers. They are drought-tolerant and long-lived additions to the Southern plant palette.

Rosa × fortuniana (Fortune, 1850)

Scottish plant explorer Robert Fortune had a keen eye for useful and beautiful Chinese plants. Among other roses he found and brought back to Europe were Fortune's double yellow and Fortune's five colored rose, as well as the famous *Rosa × fortuniana*.

Fortuniana looks like a cross between the white Lady Banks and the

Cherokee rose (*Rosa laevigata*), also known as the state flower of Georgia. Foliage is dark green and glossy. Flowers are very double, about two inches in diameter, and occur in masses. The plants are very vigorous and disease resistant. Our late friend Dr. Robert Basye, a math professor at Texas A&M who was also a serious rose breeder, felt that fortuniana was an outstanding rootstock as well.

Although fortuniana flowers and foliage are larger than those of the white Lady Banks, the two roses are often confused. That was the case for a beautiful fortuniana specimen that Mattie Rosprim had on a wire fence at the edge of her cottage garden in College Station, Texas, in the 1980s.

Mary Anne and Bob Pickens constructed beautifully proportioned cedar post arbors to support fortuniana roses at their home near Frelsburg, Texas. The fortuniana arches create a memorable picture when they bloom with the fields of bluebonnets and sheets of coreopsis in early spring. Their home is a reproduction of Pearfield Nursery (established 1876), the home of Mary Anne's grandparents (J. F. Leyendecker, 1838–1906). In addition to growing roses, Pearfield Nursery was known for fruit trees and pecans. In 1904, Leyendecker was awarded a bronze medal for his 'Le Conte,' 'Smith,' and 'Kieffer' pears. He was often first with new fruits and was known for introducing Japanese persimmons. For many years after his death the family kept the nursery going. There is more information on Pearfield Nursery in the Leyendecker Family Papers in the Barker History Collection at the University of Texas Library in Austin.

Plant explorer Robert Fortune brought back the mysterious species hybrid *Rosa × fortuniana* from China in 1850. It is a strong grower with masses of very double white flowers in the spring (image courtesy of Ralph Anderson).

'Mrs. B. R. Cant' (Cant, 1901)

'Mrs. B. R. Cant' is one of the most useful of the old roses. It is in the tea class, which further defines it as a strong repeat bloomer. The large flowers have pale, silvery-rose petals tipped with dark rose. They are very full, quartered, and fragrant. Resistance to black spot is good. My first plant was a gift from Mrs. Josephine Kennedy of Springfield, Louisiana, who had a huge specimen in her front garden. It is a favorite of hers and of everyone else I know who has grown it.

Mature plants can reach six to seven feet tall and wide. Tony Scanapico of Round Top, Texas, has a large specimen in his front garden. 'Mrs. B. R. Cant' is also nice as a large hedge and a favorite as a cut flower.

Blossoms of the tea rose 'Mrs. B. R. Cant' are pale silvery rose tipped with dark rose. Fragrance is excellent.

'Duchesse de Brabant' (Bernede, 1857)

This is a distinctive old tea rose with large, soft, rosy-pink, cupped and intensely scented flowers with forty-five petals. One of my favorite memories of it was coming upon it in a cemetery in Cuero, Texas. The plant was about three feet tall and in full bloom. It was growing on a gravesite adjacent to a pot of plastic Easter lilies. Seeing that combination always makes me smile.

'Duchesse de Brabant' was a

'Duchesse de Brabant' was a favorite rose of Teddy Roosevelt.

favorite rose of Teddy Roosevelt, who wore a bud or flower frequently as a boutonniere. A white sport of this variety, 'Madame Joseph Schwartz,' was released in 1880 and is equally valuable. It has pink tints on the edges of the petals. We have found both forms of this rose on old sites in Texas and the South.

Black spot and mildew can be a problem with this rose, but it does tend to survive. Its three- to five-foot size makes it useful in shrub masses or in containers.

Rosa laevigata (Cherokee rose, Michaux, 1803)

The Cherokee rose is unfortunately often confused with *R. bracteata*, the Macartney rose, which is a pest in Texas pastures. Georgians may be well aware of their state flower, but Cherokee is little known elsewhere in the South.

Leonard Plukenet first mentioned it botanically in 1696. It was originally noted in China and Indochina. Michaux named it in 1803 from specimens he saw in the United States, in Georgia.

The Cherokee rose is a healthy, robust climber that is spectacular in full bloom. The clean, shiny, dark green foliage and two- to three-inch, moderately fragrant, bright white spring flowers with yellow stamens make it a perfect choice for covering large trellises or climbing up trees.

It is speculated that at some point the Cherokee rose was crossed with the white form of Lady Banks, which resulted in *Rosa × fortuniana*, also a very useful, pest-free, and healthy climbing rose that needs no maintenance once established. Both of these roses satisfy today's requirement for drought- and heat-resistant landscape plants.

The Cherokee rose is another rose with a reputation for vigorous growth combined with masses of bright white blooms centered with golden stamens.

'Mermaid' (image courtesy of Mike Shoup).

'Mermaid' (Paul, 1918)

Although its parent (*Rosa bracteata*) has a bad reputation as an invasive pasture plant, Paul crossed it with a double yellow tea rose. The result became a highly regarded climbing rose of great vigor. It has glossy, disease-free foliage and is repeat flowering. It received a gold medal from the National Rose Society. The five-petaled, pale yellow flowers with amber stamens are about five inches wide. Although it needs room, support, and tolerance of its vicious thorns, 'Mermaid' is a distinctive, useful climber that is still popular today.

'Mermaid' is a popular wall rose in England in gardens such as Hampton Court, Hever Castle, and numerous other estates. Jack Harkness, a past president of the Royal National Rose Society, gives 'Mermaid' his five-star rating and lists it among the ten finest roses of all time. It thrives in Texas and the South and is only occasionally damaged by cold in those areas. It was one of the first roses grown by the Antique Rose Emporium in Independence, Texas.

'Veilchenblau' (hybrid multiflora, Schmidt, 1909)

This rose was referred to as the "blue rose" when it originated. It is a vigorous, once-blooming, climbing rose that has 'Crimson Rambler' as a parent. The nearly thornless, graceful stems completely covered with violet flowers streaked in white with yellow stamens are an unforgettable sight. This highly

When 'Veilchenblau' appeared it was considered to be a sensation. It is a vigorous climber and needs plenty of room. Violet flowers streaked with white appear in the spring.

fragrant rose created quite a sensation when introduced. The grayish blue of the flowers can be memorable when contrasted with white or pale roses. It can quickly cover tree trunks, arbors, or fences. Although it blooms only in spring, its display is spectacular and its lack of thorns is appealing.

I enjoyed growing this rose at Cricket Court, where we created large wooden arches over the entrances to the rear garden. 'Trier Rambler' (hybrid multiflora, 1904, Lambert) covered a pergola nearby. 'Trier Rambler' has thirty to fifty blooms per cluster and reblooms fairly well.

The 'Marechal Niel' specimen grafted onto *R. × fortuniana* understock from Dr. Basye was planted along a fence between these robust climbers. It never achieved the vigor I had hoped for, but the scent of those beautiful yellow blossoms remains in my memory.

"Georgetown Tea"

Georgetown, Texas, is the home of Southwestern University, the oldest university in Texas, where I spent my first two years of college. It is a beautiful town with quite a few old homes and interesting gardens. One day I was driving in an older part of town close to the fraternity house where I lived for a year when I spotted a large shrub rose on the side of a modest home that was

"Georgetown Tea" is a shrub rose with double, salmon-pink blooms and a typical tea rose fragrance.

operating as a childcare center. I asked whether I could take a few cuttings and was encouraged to do so.

The flower has been described as long budded and fully double, dark salmon pink at the center fading to lilac pink. The petals roll into points at the tips as they unfold, giving the fully open flower a starry look. The blooms have typical tea fragrance, and the foliage is extra thick and attractive. The cuttings rooted quickly and it was one that I shared with the Antique Rose Emporium. "Georgetown Tea" is a large shrub four to six feet tall and wide. It is healthy and free flowering over many seasons.

The cupped flowers of 'Monsieur Tillier' are very distinctive shades of "rosy flesh."

'Monsieur Tillier' (tea, Berenaix, 1891)

'Monsieur Tillier' is a distinctive and beautiful old tea rose. It has cupped double flowers that rebloom nicely and occur on handsome, healthy foliage throughout the growing season. Its color has been described as rosy flesh, shaded with salmon rose and purple rose.

The bottom line is that it is a distinctive color. The compact shrubs are typically four to six feet tall and round and lend themselves to more structured
designs. Even fully open flowers are more striking than those of most of the
old tea roses.

'Madame Isaac Pereire' (Bourbon, Garcon, 1881)

Lauded for its powerful perfume, 'Madame Isaac Pereire' is a very full and
sumptuous rose. The flowers are a bright rose madder color. The plant is
vigorous but thorny and not resistant to black spot. Although described in
the literature as a good fall bloomer, like many of the Bourbons grown in the
Deep South it rarely flowers after a long and plentiful spring season. It is a
classic old-fashioned Bourbon rose. Although it is important in rose literature
and is seen in Victorian gardens and catalogs, I have never observed it in an
abandoned garden.

'Madame Isaac
Pereire.'

Rubus coronarius, blackberry rose.

Blackberry rose (*Rubus coronarius*, double)

This Victorian novelty was commonly passed around old Southern gardens. It is actually a double form of blackberry. It is also known as "Easter rose." I received my start from Zada Walker, who had retired near Kirbyville, Texas. I planted it at my country place, Cricket Court. It was thought to be extinct in England for many years until a traveler found it growing in a garden in the Southern United States. The double white flowers are novelties and resemble two-inch white carnations.

Greg Grant

GROWING INTO A ROSARIAN

I was born in Tyler, Texas (one of the self-proclaimed "rose capitals" of the world), where the industry was based on fields of budded hybrid tea roses that I knew pretty much nothing about, save the dollar-each bundles of rose flowers peddled on the street corners in Tyler and Longview. My first venture into rose rustling came when I was a kid visiting my grandparents in the rural Pineywoods of Deep East Texas. Grandmother Emanis worked nonstop trying to make ends meet, but she knew I loved plants and indulged me as much as possible. With a very limited income, she didn't actually purchase any plants for me, but we certainly walked pastures, roadsides, and woods admiring those that were native there. My favorites were the grancy graybeard (*Chionanthus virginicus*), dogwood (*Cornus florida*), prairie phlox (*Phlox pilosa*), prairie nymphs (*Herbertia lahue*), and sandy-land bluebonnet (*Lupinus subcarnosus*), our original Texas state flower. I was also very interested in the "fancy" things growing in people's yards, especially in those still surviving at numerous old local home

Tyler, Texas, boasts one of the largest municipal rose gardens in the United States.

places where the former inhabitants were long gone. These carefree plants combined my love of wild and free native plants with those horticultural beauties nurtured by loving hands.

The first nonbulb to catch my attention was an old pink rambling rose that seemed to be firmly rooted at many of the former homesites in Arcadia. Some were piled on top of fencerows, while others were draped onto small trees, and some were in mounds in the middle of cow pastures, each marking a former residence. One day my Granny and I ventured to the old abandoned Burgay house in Arcadia and dug a few rooted runners along my dad's barbed-wire fencerow. We planted it on the front right corner of her car shed and feebly attempted to train it up to the front gable. We couldn't let it grow too out of control, as there were nest boxes for the hens to lay in attached to the side of the car shed. Despite its plethora of thorns and an annual spring bout of powdery mildew, we both looked forward to the clusters of baby pink flowers each spring. The Burgay house rose appeared to be the ever-popular 1901 rambler 'Dorothy Perkins,' supposedly the first popular mail-order rose in the United States.

When we moved with my high school band director father to White Oak, and then Longview, where I was raised, I inherited a white board fence

Sandy-land bluebonnet (*Lupinus subcarnosus*).

Many care-free plants survive around old home places.

'Dorothy Perkins' rambles "wild" on an overgrown fencerow.

with 'Blaze' roses planted along it. I knew nothing about roses, horticulture, or landscaping at the time. If I had, I would have embraced the existing red roses, as they worked well on the white fence with the dark green East Texas forest in the background. But as a budding inquisitive horticulturist attracted to glossy rose pictures in catalogs and magazines, I wanted to try something new. So in junior high I gave modern rose cultivation a try. Classmate Kirsten Stuber was participating in some sort of fund-raiser and sold me a bag of bare-root hybrid tea roses. I still remember the bright orange plastic bag full of hope. I planted them with little bed prep along the same fence where the 'Blaze' roses grew. It didn't take me long to realize that the leaves were always dropping with black spot and the healthy canes were diminishing in number each year. I was no landscaper either. Even if they had grown, a hodgepodge collection of gawky, different-colored rose bushes wouldn't have looked nearly as appropriate as the existing 'Blaze' roses. Before long I had a few spindly sticks poking out of the St. Augustinegrass and decided all this weekly primping and spraying I had read about wasn't for me. So I wrote roses off forever, or so I thought.

During my pre-college years, I stumbled along without roses, with two gardening books in hand—*Rodale's Encyclopedia of Organic Gardening* and *Crockett's Victory Garden*, both much-cherished gifts from my nongardening mom. I was much more consumed with my eight-by-twelve-foot fiberglass greenhouse, my amaryllis collection, and my huge vegetable garden tended with a dull red, antique Farmall Super A tractor my dad provided me. My only real stab at landscaping with roses was when my Grandmother Emanis and I planted the springtime-rustled start of the rambler 'Dorothy Perkins' on the corner of her car shed. But foolishly, I didn't even consider the 'Dorothy Perkins' a rose. It seemed more like a native wildflower to me. Bare-root, wax-dipped, hybrid tea rose bushes marketed in plastic packages were what I knew as roses. And I had failed miserably with these. So I loudly proclaimed my disdain for roses.

Spouting this opinion soon brought me public humiliation at a dinner party in Nacogdoches, Texas, hosted by my mom's best friend, Mary Beth Hagood. Mary Beth was the first real gardener that I ever knew, and she still maintains a beautiful garden to this day. Once folks find out you are majoring in horticulture or have a degree in horticulture, you can prepare yourself for a billion-plus gardening questions, no matter what the setting. As I used to tell my students in horticulture: I don't care whether you like roses, pecans, peaches, and turfgrass or not—you had better be prepared to answer multitudes of questions about them, because you will probably still be fielding them in your casket! So when one of the guests heard I was majoring in horticulture at Texas A&M University, she naturally started peppering me with gardening questions, including a plethora of unanswerable rose questions.

In Prissy to Scarlett fashion, I quickly let her know that I hated roses and knew nothing about them. Well, that just wouldn't do. She immediately attracted a giant crowd, making a fuss over this gardening nitwit who was majoring in horticulture and knew nothing about roses! It was quite a performance, with all staring at me in disbelief. So I headed back to school determined to learn more about roses.

It was at this time that Bill Welch literally changed my life when he came and spoke to one of my introductory horticulture classes at Texas A&M on the history of roses. I had never heard or seen such. He wove a fascinating story of assorted species and cultivars of roses from the beginning of humankind. He also showed picture after picture of flowers that I didn't even realize were roses. It turns out my hybrid teas and rambling rose were just two of many types of roses. But what most fascinated me in his lecture was his revelation that there were roses that grew without fertilizer, spraying, or training, and they were to be found at abandoned home places and cemeteries. Those

The chinquapin rose (*Rosa roxburghii* 'Plena') is one of many unusual rose species.

‘Old Blush’ is one of many antique roses found surviving at abandoned homes in the South.

were *my* places! I immediately went home to start searching for more of these lost treasures.

The first ones I came across were at my great-aunt Ruby Dee Smith's house. The house had actually belonged to her parents (my great-grandparents), Jake and Dee Smith. Although the locals referred to them as Mr. Jake and Miss Dee, the family called them Big Dad and Big Momma after my Grandmother Ruth and her sister Effie had children, making them "little mommas." Ruby Dee loved animals and was surrounded by cows, chickens, ducks, geese, guineas, dogs, and so forth. Except for growing vegetables to eat, she wasn't a gardener, though. Luckily, some of Big Momma's flowers held on in the yard, including three different old roses.

Out near the fence beneath some old, bright pink crapemyrtles was a surviving specimen of the same fragrant magenta-colored rose that Dr. Welch had introduced from north Louisiana as "Maggie," along with a white-

Greg's great-grandmothers Miss Eva Emanis (left) and Miss Dee Smith (Big Momma) sitting on Big Momma's front porch.

flowered rose that I call "Big Momma's Musk." This thorny, small-leaved rose has large clusters of very small, double white roses crowned with bright yellow stamens. There was also a large specimen of it just down the road at the back corner of the old Jim Crawford house, across from the Emanis house where I live now. I later found the same rose clinging to life in the New Prospect cemetery not too far away.

But without a doubt, the rose that most intrigued me at my paternal great-grandparents' old place was one that I eventually referred to as "Big Momma's Blush." My Grandmother Ruth and her sister Ruby Dee claimed that their Smith family had brought this old tea rose to Texas with them from Tennessee. I was also told that the plant I was attempting to propagate wasn't the original, which had actually been on the other side of the front yard. The one I was dealing with was a cutting-grown plant from the earlier specimen. I later found an old black-and-white snapshot with a picture of the original rose in the front yard along with Big Momma and one of my Powdrill relatives.

Big Momma admires her "Big Momma's Blush" tea rose.

I've never found a true ID or name for it, but it's as close to the Hume's blush tea scented China illustrated by Redouté as any I've ever seen, though it doesn't have a strong fragrance. It appears to me to be the same rose that Ruth Knopf found and introduced in South Carolina as "Rock Island Peach Tea." I don't consider "Big Momma's Blush" anything spectacular, but like other tea roses in the South, she is a survivor. The somewhat globular flowers have petals that are sometimes quartered (or even in bundles of twos or threes) and tend to be peachy colored during cool weather and pale pink to almost white during hot weather. And as with most tea and China roses, the new growth is burgundy colored.

I have to be honest, though. I didn't know a tea rose from a tea set until I carried samples of "Big Momma's Blush" back to Texas A&M with me to meet extension horticulturist and newfound antique rosarian Dr. Welch face to face in his office for the first time.

ROSE PROPAGATION

When I first took cuttings of "Big Momma's Blush" I didn't have access to a greenhouse, rooting hormone (Pam Puryear would have used willow water), or a mist system. From then on, access to a greenhouse and mist system became the first thing I asked about in job interviews! Sadly, none of Big Momma's cuttings rooted despite Granny Ruth's Uncle Jewel Jones sitting on the porch telling me how they used to place "heel" cuttings (those with a piece of the next stem attached) in the ground under fruit jars. But I wasn't to be deterred. The next time I came home I used the easier propagation method known as layering. I girdled or slightly broke several side branches and pinned them to the ground with old bricks I found nearby. Guess what? One rooted! I severed it from the mother plant during the fall and moved it to a new location. From that original plant I propagated more and shared them.

Creating new plants is one of the magical wonders of horticulture and is one of my greatest joys in life. Plant propagation is divided into sexual (seed) and asexual (clonal) methods. Though it's possible that they will look similar, plants produced from seed are never identical to the parent plant. Like children in a family, it's even very possible that they might look nothing like their mother or father. In the wild, roses reproduce by seed, which is contained in small apple-like fruits known as rose hips. Many hybrid roses are sterile, however, and produce no hips or seed. Growing roses from seed is best left to breeders and expert propagators, as the seed generally requires cold-moist stratification and germinates erratically.

Asexual methods of propagation include budding, grafting, cuttings, layering, and division. While many modern hybrid tea roses are produced by budding, this tedious method is also once again better left for industry experts. Clumping roses that produce numerous shoots or suckers at the ground are easily propagated by division. The entire plant can be dug with the root ball, and the crown can be cut and separated into several different plants with a sharp shovel or axe, or an individual piece can be severed from the edge of the clump by means of a "sharp-shooter" shovel. When propagating by division, it's very important that the pieces you end up with have both a portion of the root system and the aboveground stem(s). It's also very important that they be planted and watered in immediately to reduce transplant shock as much as possible. Carrying the severed crowns in a plastic trash bag sprinkled with just a bit of water inside is a good method of transporting them as long as the bag doesn't sit in the sun or get hot.

Another easy method of propagating certain roses is layering. Layering most naturally fits running or rambling roses with long, flexible stems. It can also be used on shrub roses, but it's more difficult to physically bend the stems to the ground. Layering is done by laying a stem on the ground and holding it in place with a sturdy wire pin, brick, or rock. Although it's easy to root running roses and is generally not necessary, it's often best to wound the portion of the stem that's going to be in contact with the ground. A small slice can be cut into the stem (being careful not to cut all the way through), or a small ring of bark can be girdled or removed. This wounding concentrates the natural rooting hormones in the plant and often stimulates the formation of new roots on the portion of the stem in contact with the moist ground.

By far the majority of rustled roses are propagated from cuttings. If you want to be successful in this endeavor there are some extremely important rules to follow and horticultural basics to learn. First on the list is how to handle the cuttings, as there are supplies that you will need. It's critical to keep a sharp pair of hand pruners with you for taking the cuttings. It's also extremely important to carry one-gallon plastic ziplock storage bags or something similar to store the cuttings in until you can stick them. And yes, "sticking" is a horticultural term! For every minute cuttings stay severed from the mother plant, their chances of rooting go down. But if placed in a slightly moistened plastic bag and kept cool, these cuttings don't lose any water and stay fresh for hours. Serious rose rustlers generally bring along an ice chest for storing cuttings. If placed in a refrigerator, rose cuttings can often last for weeks. I have even been known to use plastic water bottles and large soft drink bottles out of trash cans to carry my cuttings in, as they are generally already moist inside and can be capped to keep the cuttings from drying out. To heck with personal hygiene, roses always come first! DO NOT leave bagged or bottled cuttings in the bright sunlight or they will literally roast in minutes. Place them in the shade, at room temperature if you can, or preferably in air conditioning or refrigeration as soon as possible. I've seen many ill-fated cuttings dragged around in the open for hours knowing full well that they weren't going to root. With limited cuttings from very important plants I've even been known to carry them in my mouth (thorns removed of course!) like slender green cigars until I can get them to "safety."

Now let's back up and talk about what kind of cuttings to take. For most of my career I've seen novice rose propagators collect old thorny wood from spring- and fall-pruned roses to stick for cuttings. This is actually the least desirable type of cutting to take. Cutting wood can be categorized into hard wood, semihard wood, green wood, and soft wood. Always remember that younger growth has more natural rooting hormones than older growth, which makes the young wood easier to propagate. I would suggest never using old, brown, thorny hard wood, as it just doesn't root well. Which type of younger wood you use depends on how you are able to handle your cuttings and what type of propagation setup you have. Although succulent and tender new vegetation roots well if you are able to keep it from wilting, it requires "intensive care" and generally a greenhouse with a mist system. Since most potential rose gardeners don't have access to a greenhouse, just-hardened-off green wood or semihard wood (if it's your only choice) generally works best. A rule of thumb is to take recent-blooming growth, about a pencil's length and a pencil lead's girth, just after (or even weeks after) the petals have fallen off. This material is young enough to still root well but hardened off enough so as not to wilt excessively. Remember, wilting is the enemy. Four node cuttings (four sets of leaves with four total buds) are a general rule of thumb to shoot

Just-hardened-off, new green growth makes the best rose cutting wood.

for. All the leaves should be left on the cutting until it's stuck. At that time the lower set (on the portion of the stem that will be below soil level) should be removed. All the leaves that will be aboveground should be left on; they are critical to good rooting since they release their own rooting hormones.

With a greenhouse mist propagation facility and liquid rooting hormone, I often achieve 90–100 percent rooting, but at home the percentages will be much lower. Therefore it's always important to stick as many as ten times the number of cuttings you think you will need. If you root too many you can always give them away. Also be aware that some roses are fairly easy to root (ramblers), some are potentially moderately successful (teas, Chinas, and polyanthas), and some are very difficult (banksias and gallicas).

Though roses can be rooted anytime they are actively producing new growth (spring, summer, and fall), I've always thought the fall was the best time for most homeowners since the weather is beginning to moderate and is less likely to roast or dry out cuttings.

Another mistake novice gardeners make is trying to root cuttings in water. It may work a bit for ivy, coleus, sweet potatoes, and oleander, but not for roses. And even if it did, the roots produced in water are not the same as the roots produced in soil. There's not enough oxygen present in water to produce new roots. The ideal rooting media should hold half water and half air. These would include 50 percent sand with 50 percent sphagnum peat moss, 50 percent perlite with 50 percent vermiculite, or 50 percent perlite with 50 percent potting soil. At SFA we successfully used 25 percent perlite with 75 percent composted black pine bark for all of our cuttings. Remember, the key is something that holds air and moisture at the same time. Too much air means the cuttings will dry out and not root. Too much moisture means they

Greg uses a combination of 75 percent composted black pine bark and 25 percent coarse perlite to root his roses.

will rot. At SFA we also added Osmocote slow-release fertilizer (or something similar) to our rooting media to ensure vigorous growth once rooting occurs.

Then there's the question of whether to use rooting hormone or not. The answer is always yes! Rooting hormone almost always increases the rooting percentages and the rooting quality. While it's easier to find powdered hormones like Rootone and Hormodin, most nurseries use liquid hormones since more of the actual chemical goes into the cutting. The liquid hormone is also less likely to come off when the cutting is inserted into the soil media. At SFA we used concentrated Dip and Grow, which we diluted with water according to the label. Three different rates are recommended depending on the type of plant being propagated, but I use the high "woody plant" rate for everything. My original rose rustling mentor, Pam Puryear, swore by "willow water," a concoction produced by steeping cut willow twigs in water. It turns out that easy-to-root willow trees have abundant rooting hormone. I never found it nearly as effective as the concentrated commercial product, but you might want to give it a try in Pam's memory.

I use a greenhouse and an intermittent mist system to propagate roses because I have access to one with my job. Of course most gardeners don't have this luxury. It is important, however, to try to create greenhouse-like conditions for your cuttings. They must have high humidity to keep them from desiccating. This means you'll need to create your own little mini-greenhouse for your propagation bed. In the old days, would-be propagators would place a fruit jar or a cloche over their rose cuttings to hold warmth and humidity. Today this is often accomplished with old aquariums or makeshift "tents" made from clear plastic, including the thin bags that dry cleaners use to cover clean laundry. My favorite used to be a clear plastic box with a handle on top. If conditions seem too moist inside, you'll need to prop open the plastic to allow some humidity to escape. It's extremely important not to place the bed in direct sunlight, though, as the plants will literally cook to death inside. I used to use the back of a flower bed off the north end of the house that was bright but not sunny. Other friends seem to do a fine job rooting in pots on their patios, with the pots covered with plastic tents or large plastic bottles. This is certainly an option if you don't have access to open bed space. I prefer rooting in the ground, as the plants are less likely to dry out and the soil temperature is buffered, staying warmer during the winter and cooler during the summer.

Once the cuttings are stuck, it's extremely important to water them in. This seals the stems into the media by reducing air pockets. From this point on, it's important to remember that the cuttings don't actually use any water because they don't have any roots. Many cuttings rot because of overwatering. The reason professionals use an intermittent mist system is to keep the leaves moist enough that the cuttings don't lose water and dry out. Sanitation is also extremely important. Dead leaves and dead cuttings should be removed as soon as you see them. Remember, one bad apple spoils the barrel.

It generally takes about a month or so for cuttings to fully root. If they are rooted in pots, I never transplant them until roots show from the bottom of the pot and the container is full of roots. This prevents the soil from falling off the root ball during repotting or planting. The less root disturbance, the better. If the roses are in the ground, I suggest waiting two seasons to move them. Spring-rooted roses could be transplanted in the fall, and fall-rooted roses could be transplanted the following spring.

Unfortunately, all this hard work doesn't guarantee success. Diligence is the only guarantee. Remember, "if at first you don't succeed, try, and try again." As I mentioned earlier, I failed with the first rose I ever tried to propagate from cuttings. Despite my Uncle Jewel's expert coaching, my cuttings still didn't take, most likely because I used stems that were too old, let the cuttings dry out too much, didn't use rooting hormone, and didn't stick nearly enough cuttings. The next time I returned to Arcadia, I smartly pulled a lower branch to the ground, partially broke it, placed a bit of soil over it, and put an old brick on top of it. By the fall my new plant was rooted.

Once you've propagated and saved an antique rose, it's very important to share it with as many folks as possible. This helps ensure that it won't become extinct and also provides you with a source if something happens to the original plant and yours happens to die. After my "Big Momma's Blush" took root, I cut off the branch where it attached to the mother plant. The following spring I dug it and moved it to another landscape where I immediately began to propagate more cuttings. Thank goodness I did, because it wasn't long before the lone surviving plant exposed to Ruby Dee's minimal maintenance and marauding menagerie died. If I hadn't taken the time and initiative to propagate it, my family rose would have been lost forever.

ROSE ROSETTE DISEASE *Greg Grant*

I hate to be the bearer of bad news, but if you haven't already heard about it, there's a devastating virus lurking in the rose world that you absolutely must be aware of. Pay very close attention to what I'm saying here, as it could potentially end our long-standing love affair with roses. No garden roses are immune, including tough old pass-along heirlooms, no matter what they have survived in the past.

The disease is known as rose rosette and is sometimes referred to as "witches broom" because of one of its distinguishing characteristics. It was first found in Canada and Wyoming in the 1940s and appeared in Texas in the 1990s. Though it has been documented in both the Houston and San Antonio areas, it is by far most prevalent in the Dallas area, especially on the wildly popular Knock Out® roses. I have seen lots of it in roadside and public plantings in the north Dallas, McKinney, and Melissa areas. It also occurs throughout the entire South, so none of us are safe.

The symptoms of this disease are quite distinct and shouldn't be confused with anything other than herbicide damage. The most noticeable sign of this disease is a deformed, densely clustered ("witches broom") growth habit, with an abnormal bright red coloration. The plant basically goes crazy, as if it had been sprayed with 2,4-D (broadleaf) herbicide. The stems might also be flattened, enlarged, or elongated and have excessive leaf growth or thorniness. Don't confuse the burgundy-red, normal-shaped new growth of most Chinas and teas with rose rosette. And thornless roses generally won't produce excess thorniness when infected. Also be aware that the typical symptoms of rose rosette might occur on only a single or a few shoots at first, not on the entire plant. The rose may die or may linger in stunted form for years, affecting any other roses in the area.

So what causes this nightmare? Rose rosette is generally spread to other plants in two ways. In gardens and the wild it is spread by a tiny eriophyid mite that feeds on an infected plant and then spreads it to an uninfected plant that it later feeds on. These mites are so small that they can apparently be spread by the wind. But to be on the safe side, make sure roses are spaced so that they do not touch each other. Though pesky, the mite itself doesn't cause the disease. It only spreads it. The toughness of some plants, like Knock Out® roses, may keep them living longer with the disease, allowing it to spread to more and more roses nearby. The other common way of spread-

A densely clustered "witches broom" growth habit is the most noticeable sign of the incurable rose rosette disease (image courtesy of Neil Sperry).

Elongated red growth is another sign of rose rosette disease (image courtesy of Neil Sperry).

ing this deadly disease is through plant propagation. Any rose rooted from an infected plant will have the disease as well, as the virus is coursing through its sap and inner tissue. And any rose budded or grafted from an infected plant will most likely have the disease, too.

Is there a cure for this dreadful disease? Unfortunately, there isn't. Viruses are fairly common in the horticulture world—some deadly, some only slightly disfiguring, and some hardly noticeable at all. But one common trait among them is that there isn't a cure for them in your garden, no matter what quack advice or miracle remedies you hear of. I've been gardening all my life and have two degrees in horticulture. This is very common knowledge about viruses. Pruning out the noticeably infected branches won't cure a bush. Killing the mites on an infected plant won't cure it either, and neither will treating the plant or soil with assorted concoctions. By the time you see the symptoms, the disease is being replicated inside the plant and there is no way for you to get rid of it.

The *only* option you have is to completely remove and dispose of the entire plant, roots and all, when you know you have it, preferably at the very first sign of infection. If you allow an infected plant to live, you unfortunately risk the life of all your other roses along with everybody else's. I don't care how special the rose is or how much you paid for it. An infected plant, no matter how few branches seem infected, is a "Typhoid Mary" that can infect all other uninfected roses. If you remove infected plants but have other roses in the landscape, you would be wise to treat them with an appropriately labeled miticide to make sure they aren't spreading it to your other plants. It is absolutely essential for cities, municipalities, businesses, and botanical gardens to remove their infected plants, too. Otherwise, in my opinion, they are committing "crimes" against both horticulture and our beloved national flower. Do you really think civic beautification is worth it if you are killing off all other roses because of your negligence? Master Gardener groups, Master Naturalist groups, garden clubs, rose societies, and other civic-minded organizations need to be diligent about scouting their towns and gardens along with providing sound education and advice on this horrible disease. Our rose gardening heritage depends on it.

There are two very ironic side notes to this problem. First, rose rosette was originally thought to be an environmental blessing that could help rid the United States of the wildly invasive Japanese multiflora rose (*Rosa multiflora*). It was projected to kill the multiflora rose quickly, with no thought to the possibility of infecting the many beautiful garden roses in ornamental

landscapes. How many times do we think we've solved a problem only to create one even worse? Naturally, rose rosette is more common where there are naturalized stands of Japanese multiflora rose. *Rosa multiflora* has always been a common rootstock for hybrid tea roses in East Texas; therefore, there are plenty of scattered plants both sprouted from "dead" grafted roses and naturalized from the small hips spread by birds and other animals. But the numbers here don't begin to compare with the oceans of *Rosa multiflora* in other parts of the country, where it was introduced years ago for erosion control and wildlife habit. Will we ever learn? I remember seeing entire pastures full of it in rural Tennessee. It's also very common in the Virginias and Carolinas. I would strongly suggest killing or removing any *Rosa multiflora* on property that you own. Its clusters of small, blackberry-like white flowers in spring and tiny red fall hips on mounding or climbing plants are quite easy to recognize. Let this be another lesson about introducing nonnative solutions into million-year-old native ecosystems.

The other irony here is that the ever-popular and easy-to-grow Knock Out® rose was going to allow all folks, both gardeners and nongardeners alike, to grow roses. But that's what the rose rustler–antique rose movement was for! We already had a good answer, at least for the South, with teas and Chinas. But just as copycat gardeners did with Bradford pear, red-tipped photinia, and now loropetalum, they got carried away with endless stands of

Large beds of Knock Out® roses mark many commercial and civic landscapes today.

Knock Out® roses. Planting one kind of plant exclusively has never been a good thing. It sets the stage for mass infection from insects or disease. Dutch elm disease took care of streets lined with American elm, and entomosporium leaf spot took care of hedges of red-tipped photinia as far as the eye could see. Diversity is always a good thing, in nature and in gardens. Since particular insects and diseases generally infect only certain plants, diversity helps keep the problem from spreading and devastating entire populations. I hate to say it, but I would not recommend large mass plantings of any rose, particularly in areas that aren't highly managed or monitored. This is where rose rosette is lurking and spreading at the moment.

I would also be very diligent not only in removing all infected roses but also in propagating or purchasing new plants. Rose plantings near naturalized stands of *Rosa multiflora* along with those in highly developed urban areas heavily planted with roses are most at risk. Do all you can to stop the spread of this disease. I do not want to hear Willie Nelson's "Turn Out the Lights, the Party's Over" echoing in my mind in roseless gardens of the future.

THE SEARCH FOR THE
SAN ANTONIO ROSE

I worked with Bill Welch and Mike Shoup at the new Antique Rose Emporium until I finished graduate school. My first real job after that took me to Alston's Nursery on Ninth Avenue in Port Arthur, Texas, formerly Eagleson's Nursery. The late Mr. Eagleson was well known for camellia breeding and his heavily berried *Ilex × attenuata* 'Eagleson' holly hybrid, which I still grow. One morning while driving to work I couldn't help but notice a rose in full bloom on one end of a small frame house. The glorious pink tea rose was larger than the house! It just happened to be 'Duchesse de Brabant,' one of the few that I could actually identify. It's still one of my favorites to this day.

After a short stint in Port Arthur, I accepted the county horticulturist

'Duchesse de Brabant.'

position in San Antonio in 1987. In addition to history, great Mexican food, and the beautiful River Walk, San Antonio was home to a plethora of old roses and I wanted to see them all. To facilitate this desire, with the help of local area extension horticulturist Dr. Jerry Parsons, we came up with "The Search for the San Antonio Rose." While most folks have known for years that the Yellow Rose of Texas and San Antonio Rose were women, not roses, I still wanted to use the popularity of the legendary songs to promote our contest. With the help of KENS-TV and corporate sponsor Miller Beer, we offered a $500 cash prize for the oldest documented rose in San Antonio. Through television, radio, and newspaper, we encouraged people to search their gardens, farms, cemeteries, and family histories for any and all Texas-tough heirloom roses still in existence. The idea was to find out which roses truly liked growing in San Antonio and to use this information to help guide future rose cultivation there.

And, oh, were there some beauties. The most common pass-along rose in San Antonio turned out to be the 1907 tea 'Mrs. Dudley Cross.' Because

The beautiful 'Mrs. Dudley Cross' that gave her life for the Alamodome in San Antonio.

Pam Puryear, Greg Grant, and Bill Welch get interviewed about Mrs. Adlair's good-looking 'Mrs. Dudley Cross' roses.

of its completely smooth stems, one local resident even referred to it as "the rubber stemmed rose." One of the most beautiful specimens of all was, unfortunately, on the future site of the Alamodome and was destroyed when construction began. While judging the entries with invited experts Dr. Welch and Pamela Ashworth Puryear, we stumbled across several glorious 'Mrs. Dudley Cross' tea roses in full bloom at Mary Adlair's Canton Street home on the east side of San Antonio. Since we had Dr. Parsons and a local television crew with us, we decided to interview her to find out what she had done to produce the prettiest roses in San Antonio.

I remember that she seemed a bit embarrassed about all the fuss and finally confessed that she had done absolutely nothing to the roses to deserve any praise. All the credit belonged to the crew painting the house, who had simply cut them to the ground with a chain saw, stimulating them to spring forth with new growth and bountiful flowers. That was it? No watering? No insecticide and fungicide every seven to ten days? No special rose fertilizer? No scraping the bud union and cutting back spent blooms to the first set of five leaflets? This was *exactly* the kind of rose I was looking for! I was in love. Anybody could do this.

Another beautiful specimen of 'Mrs. Dudley Cross' survived in front of a large abandoned two-story house in the historic King William District, where

A beautiful specimen of 'Mrs. Dudley Cross' in front of a two-story home in San Antonio's King William District.

I lived at the time. Early one morning, I awoke to the sounds of sirens and neighbors rushing up and down the sidewalk. The large old house where Mrs. Dudley lived was engulfed in a four-alarm blaze and everybody was worried about it spreading to the many beautifully restored homes in the neighborhood. Of course my first thought was about the rose bush, not the burning house. So while others were running down the street screaming "Save our houses!" I filed right in behind them screaming "Save Mrs. Dudley!"

The house was a total loss, and several weeks later I strolled by to observe the devastation. There was only *one* thing left on the entire property—a large specimen of 'Mrs. Dudley Cross' with half of the bush blackened from the fire and the other half in full bloom. The fire was simply one more inconvenience in her life's quest for glory. Hooray for tenacity. Because 'Mrs. Dudley Cross' was so adapted and so common, we eventually gave her the honorary title of "The San Antonio Rose" and encouraged her planting throughout the historical city.

There were many other fine specimens and entries as well. One that comes to mind was a pair of 'Louis Philippe' (1834) China roses tangled with native chile pequin peppers in front of an abandoned house on Pine Street. Old roses, a beer sponsor, and hot peppers—this was Texas rose rustling at its best! These tough, east-side China roses were what I consider the true

A scorched
'Mrs. Dudley
Cross' survived a
four-alarm blaze
and a horde of
firefighters.

'Mrs. Dudley
Cross' was
so prolific
and common
throughout San
Antonio that she
was given the
honorary title of
"The San Antonio
Rose."

A pair of 'Louis Philippe' roses thrived at an abandoned home just east of downtown San Antonio.

'Louis Philippe' that produced fully double red roses, airbrushed with white in the center, on vigorous large shrubs. Most of what Southern gardeners have obtained over the last several decades is an imposter, in my opinion, that is probably the redder, hollow-centered, more delicate 'Cramoisi Superieur' or something similar. It appears to me that this mix-up first occurred at the Antique Rose Emporium and was spread throughout the country. My first plant of the real 'Louis' came from Pam Puryear and I still grow a specimen of it.

Another interesting find was a seventy-five-year-old specimen of a different thornless tea rose at the Army Street home of a Mrs. Villarreal that was planted by her mother. It had pale yellow flowers that became almost white in hot weather. I still grow and enjoy it to this day and occasionally grew it for our plant sales as the "Satin Cream Tea." On later trips to San Antonio I also found it in other west-side gardens. It occasionally sets a few seed, so I've always wanted to start a thornless breeding project with her. I do love thornless roses. But remember what Abraham Lincoln once said: "We can complain because rose bushes have thorns, or rejoice because thorn bushes have roses."

Greg propagated what he calls the "Satin Cream Tea" from Mrs. Villarreal's seventy-five-year-old specimen.

One that really piqued our interest was what appeared to be a gallica rose in a garden off Broadway Street, just north of downtown. It was a suckering, once-blooming rose that produced beautiful, flat, fully double magenta roses. Here, Mrs. Hopper said it was a gift to her family in the 1930s from their gardener, whose family originally brought it to San Antonio from the Canary Islands. I dubbed it the "Canary Island Gallica." The Antique Rose Emporium offered it for a number of years. Interestingly enough, the original settlers in San Antonio were from the Canary Islands. To keep it more compact and to induce more flowers, Mrs. Hopper faithfully pruned it to waist height after each spring's grand display. I hope it's still around, as I'd like to grow it in my garden.

I once stopped to admire another mystery rose nearby. It was a glorious bright pink Bourbon-tea type in full bloom next to a small white frame house. The listless young man on the porch railed with castaway wooden pallets was smoking marijuana. When I asked about the rose all he had to offer was that it belonged to his mother. He and the rose both seemed very pleased in their

The "Canary Island Gallica" rose.

current states of mind. It was more testimony to the toughness of antique roses.

Another mystery rose was located at the home of Mr. Eddie Fanick, owner of the famed Fanick's Nursery on the southeast side of San Antonio. Mr. Fanick and his son John ran the nursery (along with the entire extended family) and were very dear friends of mine. Unfortunately, both have now passed away. The interesting climbing tea-Noisette was located on the side of "Old Man Fanick's" small frame house. They told me they used to sell it years

Greg, Mrs. Hopper, and Pam inspect Mrs. Hopper's pruning job on her "Canary Island Gallica" roses (image courtesy of Jerry Parsons).

ago as the "Pink Marechal Niel" rose. Later, Marion Brandes, one of the early Texas Rose Rustlers, tentatively identified it as the 1889 German-bred tea-Noisette 'Kaiserine Friedrich.' This would make sense, since San Antonio was home to one of the largest German populations in early Texas. However, other experts with extensive knowledge of heirloom roses

strongly suggest that it is the 1895 tea-Noisette 'E. Veyrat Hermanos,' which they say is an "overly vigorous thug." The Fanick rose is an extremely vigorous climber with creamy yellow flowers airbrushed with hot pink when the weather is cool. Though it has some problems with balling (petals sticking together and preventing the flower from opening) during the spring, I grow it on the back of my henhouse and think fondly of the Fanicks when it blooms. As with people, no roses are perfect, nor do I expect them to be. Like all teas and their kin, she's quite a spectacle in the fall, however. Though this rose is not related to the legendary yellow-flowered climber 'Marechel Niel,' one can see how its superficial resemblance and pink tones earned it the pass-along name "Pink Marechal Niel."

The ultimate winner of our contest was something from the near–west side of San Antonio that Mr. Everett Cockrell's family called the "Old English Tea Rose," though it certainly wasn't a tea rose. It appeared to be 'Louise Odier' and was documented on the site at 101 years old. Interestingly enough, it had been "fertilized" through the years by the deceased family cats buried around it. Thanks to corporate sponsor Miller Beer, we awarded an ecstatic Mr. Cockrell a check for $500 for having the oldest documented rose in San Antonio. This same house on Commerce Street was called "The

Greg inhaled as he photographed this beautiful mystery rose just north of downtown San Antonio.

Eddie Fanick and his family at the legendary Fanick's Nursery in San Antonio.

Fanick's "Pink Marechal Niel."

An ecstatic Mr. Cockrell earned a check for $500.

Lamarque Cottage" for the then ninety-nine-year-old climber growing at the front door. We were told that friends and relatives from the North always marveled that the creamy white rose trained over the entrance was still in bloom during the Thanksgiving and Christmas holidays. Now whether this rose was actually the 1830 Noisette 'Lamarque' or not is another question, for it wasn't the same as the one being sold by the Antique Rose Emporium.

The Lamarque Cottage rose did appear to be identical to a large rose growing next to a small stucco house on Flores Street, as I propagated both and grew them side by side. As this Flores Street rose continued to grow and the house continued to decline, it was later dubbed the "Flores Street House Eater Rose" by curious Texas Rose Rustlers who came across it. Unfortunately, both the house and vigorous climber are now gone, but thanks to the Texas Rose Rustlers I still grow the rose. I have different photographs of the rose when it is modest sized, starting to cover the house, and completely covering the house.

The famed "Flores Street House Eater" rose.

A true seven sisters rose and 'Old Blush' survive at an abandoned home in Round Top, Texas.

Many roses in the contest were referred to as the rose of Castille and seven sisters, though none ever turned out to be either of these legendary antique roses. The only surviving true seven sisters rose (*Rosa multiflora platyphylla*) I ever ran across was at a small abandoned cottage in Round Top, Texas, where it grew next to the original old China 'Old Blush.' There were many, many surviving roses in South Texas, an area that receives around twenty-five inches of annual rainfall and is prone to severe heat and drought. I soon learned that though they didn't thrive under these harsh conditions, it generally took a second year of serious drought to kill an existing unirrigated rose. Established antique roses are much tougher than most realize.

GREG'S OTHER RUSTLED ROSES

I'm *still* an active rustler. Many of my plant introductions have even been rustled. John Fanick phlox (*Phlox paniculata* 'John Fanick') came from a friendly elderly lady's house on Rigsby Street in San Antonio. "Pam's Pink" honeysuckle (*Lonicera × americana* "Pam's Pink") came from Pam Puryear's grandmother's former house in Navasota, Texas. Henry and Augusta Duelberg sages (*Salvia farinacea* 'Henry Duelberg' and 'Augusta Duelberg') came from a cemetery not far from La Grange, Texas. Peppermint Flare rose mallow (*Hibiscus moscheutos* 'Peppermint Flare') was a sport from a hibiscus in a Nacogdoches, Texas, landscape. Lecompte chaste tree (*Vitex agnus-castus* 'Lecompte') came from an old landscape in the little Louisiana town of the same name. The Nacogdoches rose (*Rosa × hybrida* "Grandma's Yellow") came from the Old Stone Fort Motel in Nacogdoches, while the climbing sport of 'Belinda's Dream' rose

Henry Duelberg sage (*Salvia farinacea* 'Henry Duelberg').

(*Rosa × hybrida* 'Farmer's Dream') came from the Rose Gardens in Farmers Branch. And the Marie Daly rose (*Rosa × polyantha* 'Marie Daly') came from my mom's backyard in Shelby County, Texas.

'Tausendschon'

One rose I recall rustling came by accident, as I didn't even see it growing in a garden. After I met with Dr. Welch about my "Big Momma's Blush" samples back in college, he soon had me working at the not yet opened Antique Rose Emporium as well as joining the fledgling Texas Rose Rustlers group. It wasn't long before there was a meeting of such enthusiasts in the horticulture building on the Texas A&M University campus. A number of found antique roses were brought to the meeting by folks for show-and-tell or identification. One happened to be a thornless multiflora rambler that nobody was able to ID. These particular snippets made their way to the back of the room, where I adopted them and decided they needed a home. Somehow I rooted one and eventually planted it back at my grandmother's home in Arcadia, where it soon covered the side of my late Papaw's old lean-to car shed.

By searching through books and catalogs I eventually decided that the

'Tausendschon' multiflora rambler.

pass-along rambler from the Texas A&M rose meeting was the German multiflora rambler 'Tausendschon,' introduced in 1906. The name means "thousand beauties," as the clusters of semidouble flowers range in all shades from white to bright pink. I confirmed its identity by growing its dwarf ever-blooming sport 'Echo' (Lambert, 1914), which has identical foliage and flower clusters.

But somewhere along the way, Dr. Welch shared a thornless rambler with me that he had acquired from an Austin garden, and he was calling *it* thousand beauties. It was obvious, however, that the Austin rose was quite different. It had smaller, shinier leaves and clusters of smaller, more double flowers in hot pink only. It was a classic wichuraiana rambler, in my opinion. To this day I haven't come up with its true name, but I tabbed it "Queenie" years ago after Dr. Welch's late wife, Diane. She was a dear friend of mine, so I figured her nickname belonged on a rose I loved. Because the "Queenie" rose grew just like 'Dorothy Perkins,' didn't have mildew or thorns, and had brighter, showier flowers, I grubbed out Miss Dorothy along the car shed and replaced her with Miss Queenie, who still resides there to this day. Although she is just a once bloomer, I dearly look forward to her hot-pink spectacle each spring. We sold her periodically at the famous annual SFA Gardens plant sales at Ste-

"Queenie" rambler.

'Veilchenblau'
multiflora rambler.

phen F. Austin State University in Nacogdoches along with many of the other
plants and new introductions from my home garden and past travels.

'Veilchenblau'

I was obviously stuck in the rambler mode for a time because I also remember stumbling across another one while still working at the Antique Rose
Emporium. It came courtesy of my Grandmother Ruth. My paternal grandfather, Hoya Doice Grant, died before I was born, and my Granny Ruth remar-
ried Andrew Mena. The Menas were Spanish Creoles from across the border
in Louisiana like my Ximines ancestors. I knew Andrew because he was one
of the fellows who played weekly dominoes with my maternal grandfather,
Rebel Eloy Emanis, and Uncle Jewel. Andrew's brother's wife in Center
contacted me about an odd rose in their backyard, so I went to check it out
that spring. It was the most unusual color I had ever seen in a rose, and I
brought a bouquet back to the Rose Emporium, where I was working on the
weekends. At the time, nobody had any idea what it was. It later proved to be
the mostly thornless 'Veilchenblau,' a 1909 German-bred multiflora rambler.
'Veilchenblau' means "violet blue." In the past, it was also known as "the blue
rose." The last time I checked, the Antique Rose Emporium was still offering it. It gets a little more black spot than I prefer, but the incredible flowers

make up for it. In my opinion, it has more color variations than the true seven sisters rose, as 'Veilchenblau' has shades of purple, blue, lavender, pink, and gray highlighted with streaks of white.

'Fragrant Snowflake'

As a student, I can remember hearing Dr. Welch talk about retired Texas A&M math professor Dr. Robert Basye and his myrrh-scented roses. Dr. Basye bred roses in nearby Caldwell for fifty years with a particular interest in black spot resistance, thornless canes, and improved rootstocks. I first met Dr. Basye at the 1989 Heritage Rose Foundation Symposium in College Station. I remember how honored I was when he came up and introduced himself after my "In Praise of the Forgotten Chinas" lecture and told me it was the best talk he had heard. The list of speakers was incredible, including legendary rose experts Pam Puryear, Virginia Hopper, Ruth Knopf, Mike Shoup, Charles Walker, and Malcom Manners. However, my pride was wounded recently when I found an old schedule for the symposium showing that I was first on the program. That means mine was the only talk he had heard when he said I was the best! Dr. Basye and I corresponded by letter for a number of years after that and he invited me to his home in Caldwell, where I visited him on several occasions.

'Fragrant Snowflake' Lady Banks.

On one visit we walked his mostly abandoned field of trial plants and seedlings. I've always loved plots given little to no care, as they quickly reveal which plants have the vigor and toughness to grow and survive on their own. In the back of the field I noticed a short row of mounding healthy green foliage and asked what it was. He explained that it was a white Lady Banks rose he had grown from seed obtained from Italy and allowed me to take cuttings back to San Antonio, where I rooted them.

In an article Dr. Basye wrote for the *American Rose Annual* in 1988 titled "A Thornless Form of Fortuniana," he provided more clues to its purpose:

> *Fortuniana* is thought to have originated as the cross, R. *banksiae* × R. *laevigata*, species which are both native to southern China. To test this assumption and perhaps recreate *Fortuniana* in a thornless form (mainly to serve as an improved understock), I needed R. *banksiae* in its thornless form. I soon acquired the double white and double yellow forms, easily found since they are superbly attractive as landscape plants in the South. They are both thornless. But they are essentially sterile. I needed *R. banksiae* in its single, thornless form.

Basye's search for a single thornless banksia led him to Father George Schoener's rose collection at the University of Santa Clara in California. Unfortunately, Father Schoener didn't have it in his collection, but he said that he had shared it with the reclusive Carmelite Convent a few blocks away. After dicey negotiations to be allowed access, it turned out to be a double-flowered banksia instead. But he didn't give up, and in his article he goes on to say:

> Knowing of no other likely source of *R. banksiae* in America, my thoughts turned to the Italian and French Rivieras. I knew that banksias flourished there and that *Fortuniana* was a favorite understock. I wrote a letter to Domenico Aicardi, the Italian rose breeder who produced Rome Glory, Signora, and Eternal Youth. This kindly old gentleman, then in his upper seventies, responded by sending me a generous handful of *banksiae* seeds, which must have taken him several hours to extract from the very small hips of *banksiae*. I have never forgotten his generosity.
>
> I was soon to learn that the seeds of *banksiae*, like those of *laevigata*, will rarely germinate the first winter after harvest and must be held over till the following winter. Among the Aicardi seedlings some were single

white, some double white, some single yellow and some double yellow. About half were thornless. And some were both single and thornless.

Starting in 1969, through several generations of crosses, Dr. Basye went on to use one of these new single thornless white banksias to produce his 85-04 'Thornless Fortuniana' rootstock, which he bred in 1984.

I took cuttings of Dr. Basye's single white banksia with me as a historical curiosity and later planted it in my garden in Arcadia. Though not as showy as the double white Lady Banks, it is the most fragrant rose I've ever grown. I once read that the Chinese name for the species noted its fragrance, which could be smelled for miles. I later named Dr. Basye's seedling 'Fragrant Snowflake' and also sold it at our SFA Gardens plant sales.

'Marechal Niel'

My San Antonio years were very prolific when it came to roses. Dr. Welch and the Texas Rose Rustlers were responsible for yet another very interesting find. They had noticed a yellow climbing rose on the back wall of a home in Bryan and thought it might be the legendary 'Marechal Niel.' This fragrant 1864 buttery yellow tea-Noisette was arguably the most popular rose of its day. This one belonged to a Mrs. Opersteny. Dr. Welch contacted her and delicately talked her into sharing cuttings with us. He arranged for us to visit.

Mrs. Opersteny's 'Marechal Niel' rose trained on the back of her Bryan, Texas, home.

I was to take the cuttings back to San Antonio and propagate them. When we arrived I went to the back of the house to photograph the rose and take cuttings while he was at the front door talking to Mrs. Opersteny. While I was in the very act of taking the cuttings, it turns out the crusty little Polish gal changed her mind and told him if she gave cuttings to him she'd have to give cuttings to everybody else who admired it. Reaching into his bag of diplomatic negotiation skills, he resorted to offering to purchase them. She relented and agreed that would work. Little did they both know that the cuttings were taken before the deal was reached! How was I to know they were haggling at the front door?

At the time, I was growing 'Marechal Niel' from Roses of Yesterday and Today in California. Everybody said it was a weak grower, and

Mrs. Opersteny's 'Marechal Niel' grafted onto a Lady Banks rose covered most of the front eave of Greg's little house in San Antonio.

sure enough, it was. As a matter of fact, most of the nineteenth-century Texas nursery catalogs offered it as a grafted plant using a vigorous rootstock to promote strong growth. It's the only old rose I've ever grown that needed to be grafted. I was instructed to send cuttings of both to Malcom Manners with the Citrus Institute at Florida Southern College, which I did. It turned out that the California plant had numerous forms of virus living in it and the Texas plant did not. Malcom grafted it onto *Rosa × fortuniana* and said it was one of the most vigorous roses he had ever grown. I normally prefer to grow roses on their own roots, but after reading and observing that this cultivar was weak rooted I decided to try budding it onto a Lady Banks rose rootstock. That certainly did the trick. On one side of my little east-side San Antonio cottage I had a several-year-old own-root plant that didn't even reach the eaves. On the other side I planted the plant budded onto yellow Lady Banks and in one year it grew up to the eaves, all the way across the house, and down to the plant on the other side. It was quite showy. That small house that I rented from Mr. Peterson at Peterson Brothers Nursery for one dollar a month provided one of my all-time favorite gardens. It had a tiny kidney-bean-shaped lawn that I could mow in five minutes and was home to my hymenocallis and crinum collections in addition to myriad other showy plants in both winter and summer. It's the little garden where I first made the crosses that would produce the dwarf pink Mexican petunia (*Ruellia brittoniana* 'Bonita'), the only plant patent with my name on it.

Although it was historically very significant, the famous 'Marechal Niel' rose was continually plagued with thrips and balling in San Antonio and provided a source of constant consternation to friend and mentor Dr. Parsons, who helped me propagate and save it. I hope Malcom Manners will share this rose back with me, as I'd like to grow her again for old time's sake.

Greg still grows the beautiful orange cross vine he named 'Helen Fredel.'

'Helen Fredel'

One of the side benefits of Mrs. Opersteny's location was that Dr. Welch also noticed a showy vine growing on the front fence of her neighbor Helen Fredel. After all, we rose rustlers know how to rustle other plants as well. Fredel was a ninety-plus-year-old retired schoolteacher. Bill said her vine looked like a hybrid between a cross vine (*Bignonia capreolata*) and a trumpet creeper (*Campsis radicans*) and sent me a

Helen Fredel shows Greg her pink tea rose in Bryan, Texas.

slide in the mail. It was very showy, with large orange flowers. Like all good academics, Dr. Welch sent me to the field to propagate it. So I drove to Bryan and met the sweetest little woman who ever lived. She was quite the contrast to her curmudgeonly neighbor Mrs. Opersteny and immediately offered me cuttings. It turned out to be a unique cross vine that she had rescued from a neighbor's house years ago. She said the cross vine had originally covered the walls of a two-story house. All the neighbors wanted cuttings, but the owners wouldn't share. Eventually the house had to be painted and the vine was stripped off the walls and piled on the side of the street. This was Mrs. Fredel's chance. She helped herself to the cast-aside cuttings and propagated her own, which thrived on the chain-link fence on both sides of her front yard. It was fortunate that she saved it, as the original house and plants were long gone. Up until this point, the only cross vine I was familiar with was the native buttery yellow form with burgundy highlights in the throat. Mrs. Fredel's selection, which I named 'Helen Fredel,' is larger flowered and intermediate in color between *atrosanguinea* and 'Tangerine Beauty,' which were just finding their way into cultivation. All were much showier than the common form in the woods.

Mrs. Fredel was also a rose lover and shared cuttings of what I still call "Bryan Fredel" tea, which appears similar if not identical to 'Maman Cochet' (1893). She said that although she had long admired it, Mrs. Opersteny wouldn't share her 'Marechal Niel' with her, either! Dear Mrs. Fredel also blessed me with crinums, Byzantine gladiolus, and Chinese ground orchids. I'll always remember her sweetness and generosity. She wrote me occasional letters until her death.

"Scottsville Gallica"

Mr. Umphress takes a break from mowing the beautiful Scottsville Cemetery near Marshall, Texas.

I was led to another rose rustle through a book on East Texas I picked up at a San Antonio used book store. I've collected books on East Texas all my life. One chapter told the story of a rose brought to the Scottsville community (near Marshall) from Mississippi and planted in 1834. For years, family reunions gathered around the still-surviving rose, and of course I wondered if it was still alive. If so, it could be the oldest rose bush in Texas! So I loaded up the truck one day and headed to Scottsville, just north of I-20, in

Once in a blue moon the "Scottsville Gallica" has blue tinges in her fragrant flowers.

northeast Texas. The first thing I found was the prettiest cemetery in Texas, with beautiful monuments and a stone chapel on-site. Sitting on some curbing in a full sweat from mowing was a Mr. Umphress. I politely explained my odd search, thinking he would shun such craziness and proceed back to mowing. But without hesitation he told me to turn right leaving the cemetery, turn right at the next driveway, pull up to the cedar tree, and the rose would be on my left. He also told me to help myself to a start if I wanted. I asked him how on earth he knew about the rose and he replied, "Because I live there." Apparently Mr. Umphress was the last person left in Scottsville and knew *all*. I did proceed up the driveway and found a suckering "gallica-type" rose surviving under an old cedar tree. The cedar trees had once been planted in an allée leading up to the old plantation house. If not for its suckering, multistemmed growth habit I doubt it would have survived all those years, especially with grass growing up to it beneath the dense shade of an eastern red cedar. I severed one of the suckers and brought it back to the SFA Mast Arboretum in Nacogdoches and planted it in the little heritage garden. It's just a once bloomer and not the easiest rose to root. Most old European-type

ROSES IN CEMETERIES *Greg Grant*

If the dead can grow them, you can too.

I've always loved cemeteries. Heck, you are going to spend more time in one
than in your home, so you might as well learn to love them as well. If you
think they are cold, lifeless places full of heartache and "haints," you are dead
wrong.

I can thank both of my grannies along with Pam Puryear for my love of
graveyards. My grandmothers introduced me to my relatives in both the Powdrill and Pleasant Grove Cemeteries near my rural home in the Pineywoods
of East Texas. They also introduced me to such cemetery etiquette as not
stepping on or standing on top of somebody's grave. Pam, on the other hand,
introduced me to cultural and horticultural history in cemeteries. Cemeteries
are truly open books written in a dead language. Their stories might be cryp-
tic, but once you learn to read them, you will be drawn to them forever.

In his fascinating book *Texas Graveyards: A Cultural Legacy* (University
of Texas Press, 1982), author Terry G. Jordan writes, "Nowhere else, I maintain, is it possible to look so deeply into our people's past. No better place
exists to ponder questions of cultur[al] history and ancient ancestral cultural
hearths. In more ways than one, we are closer to our forefathers when tread-
ing upon the ground where they lie buried."

The traditional Southern cemetery served not only as a resting place
for deceased loved ones, but as a garden of roses and other heirloom plants
as well. Interesting horticultural treasures of all kinds were planted in the
cemeteries of the past. Many had former pagan and current religious conno-
tations, such as evergreens, which symbolized eternal life. Anything remotely
resembling a lily was considered a flower of death, including crinums, amaryllis, lycoris, oxblood lilies, hymenocallis, daylilies, narcissus, daffodils, jonquils,
iris, tuberoses, and true lilies. These "lilies" were originally symbols of the
ancient Mediterranean "great mother" and later came to symbolize the Virgin
Mary. Other common Southern cemetery plants included crapemyrtles, nan-
dinas, boxwoods, red cedars, and of course roses, the Queen of them all.

It was once a custom to plant a deceased loved one's favorite plant on
his or her grave. And a particular beloved family rose often ranked number
one. Long after their garden popularity waned, many of these heirloom roses
clung to life in our older cemeteries. Oftentimes these cemeteries were the
only source of long-lost rose cultivars. A number of these cemetery roses have

been rescued and reintroduced to the nursery trade and into today's rose garden. Dr. Welch's foolproof "Natchitoches Noisette," which he propagated from the old American Cemetery in Natchitoches, Louisiana, is a fine example.

Oxblood lilies (*Rhodophiala bifida*) bloom around Greg's great-great-grandfather's headstone.

These antique roses survived and were often rediscovered in cemeteries because as a rule they are tougher and longer lived than most modern roses. I have personally seen heirloom tea and China roses thriving in cemeteries next to dying modern hybrid tea roses. It's almost like they are completely different plants, apples versus oranges. Although the blossoms aren't as showy on the antiques, any bloom on a living plant tends to outshine those on a dead plant. After all, any color looks pretty next to brown. A statement I made years ago is often repeated by fans of cemetery survivors, and it's true: if the dead can grow them, you can too!

Another reason these living antiques tended to survive in old cemeteries is that they were rooted cuttings, grown on their own roots instead of being budded onto a different understock, as modern roses have been for years. This means that after a killer freeze or after the person on the mower ran over it or girdled it with a string trimmer, the very same rose sprouted back from the ground, instead of a rambling, once-blooming rootstock.

The needs of roses in cemeteries, or any garden for that matter, are fairly simple and predictable. First and foremost they need full sun. "Full sun" means a full day's sun, not direct sun for two hours in the afternoon when the sun stops hiding behind the trees. Anybody who tells you a rose is shade tolerant is either a liar or a salesperson. And for a rose to survive in a cemetery, it absolutely must have protection from the maintenance person or crew. This means you have to hide them behind something, beside something, or between things in order to avoid mowers, string trimmers, tractors, trucks, hearses, and herbicide. Good places to plant them are next to and between headstones, out of the way of the mower. The best place of all to plant a rose or other flowers in a cemetery is on a grave surrounded by curbing, which keeps the mower and other traffic out completely. I call cemetery gardening inside the raised curbing "raised dead gardening." In more-open areas I have found that staking them with steel T-posts or sturdy rebar helps, as does keeping an all-important circle around them mulched and weed-free. The mulch helps the plants survive by keeping the soil cooler during the summer

Curbing protects this beautiful gallica rose in a cemetery in William Penn, Texas.

and warmer during the winter while keeping weeds from growing next to them, which not only compete for moisture and nutrients but also attract the person with the deadly mower and string trimmer. I frequently find surviving old roses in cemeteries with seedling trees sprouting up beside them and sometimes entirely shading them. It's absolutely essential to makes sure squirrels or Mother Nature doesn't take over your rose. This often means occasional careful work with a handsaw or a pair of loppers. I've also seen rose specimens existing beneath umbrellas of aggressive vines like Japanese honeysuckle, which can eventually choke them out if not carefully eradicated.

Even though some of the most beautiful rose specimens I've ever seen haven't been pruned, fertilized, or watered in decades or more, an ideal rose caretaker would give ever-blooming roses a light, twice-a-year shearing around each Valentine's and Labor Day, while also removing any dead branches or canes. A sprinkling of general lawn or garden fertilizer would also help them prevail over their human and botanical competition. And though

This red China rose refuses to yield to an ash tree in an Alabama cemetery.

not always feasible, a deep soaking with water once a month during a drought would also give them a leg up.

Dr. Welch and I have both added some of our favorite rustled roses to our family cemeteries. They sure beat the heck out of dead roses or gaudy plastic flowers. In my opinion, it's a crime that some cemeteries now ban living plant material. Who, pray tell, can argue against beautiful, low-maintenance, living, breathing roses and other plants in a cemetery? Are hallowed cemeteries really supposed to glow with artificial plastic by-products of the petrochemical industry? Sadly, the tradition of planting beloved plants on loved ones' graves is dying along with many cultivars of historical roses.

Luckily, a few devoted fans of old roses have taken the bull by the horns and reintroduced many of these old garden roses back to their rightful place in Southern cemeteries. Others have helped save and preserve existing antique roses in cemeteries so that future generations can enjoy their beauty and historical significance.

The Old City Cemetery in Sacramento, California; Old City Cemetery

Unfortunately, artificial flowers adorn most cemeteries across America today.

in Lynchburg, Virginia; and Greenwood Cemetery in Jackson, Mississippi, are all examples where local rosarians and volunteers have collected and preserved antique roses in a cemetery garden setting. In the Greenwood Cemetery in Jackson, where famous Southern author (and gardener) Eudora Welty is buried, good friend and legendary horticulturist Felder Rushing has amassed a collection of hundreds of antique roses that survive with almost no additional care. Every Southern town should set aside at least one local cemetery for historical and found roses in the area. After all, roses and cemeteries are a match made in heaven.

A beautiful Cherokee rose (*Rosa laevigata*) graces a brick wall in Virginia's Lynchburg Old City Cemetery.

Greg found this dark pink *Rosa multiflora* and several lighter pink seedlings around it in a field in Tennessee.

roses don't thrive in our hot, muggy climate, but despite a bit more black spot than I'd prefer, I look forward to the deeply fragrant, multipetaled magenta blooms of my "Scottsville Gallica" each spring in my home garden. Some years they are magically flushed with blue.

Pink *Rosa multiflora*

Another interesting find occurred while I was still working for the Agricultural Extension Service in San Antonio. My coworker Dr. Jerry Parsons, along with former Bexar County horticulturist Steve George and I, took a long, grueling ride to South Carolina for the Extension Triennial Workshop. Despite our friendship, none of us were speaking to each other by the time we arrived! On the way home we decided to swing through Tennessee to visit legendary nurseryman Don Shadow. Much of Tennessee is unfortunately choked with invasive *Rosa multiflora*, which has clusters of small white blackberry-like flowers. Then out of the blue (or pink in this case), I noticed a bright pink one among them and several showier lighter pinks that appeared to be seedlings nearby. I wanted to stop, but Dr. George was in a hurry to get back home. The three of us hadn't wanted to speak to each other on the way there, but by this time we didn't even want to be in the same vehicle together (note to self: three strong personalities belong in three separate vehicles)!

When we arrived at Don Shadow's nursery, Jerry told him about the pink multiflora roses I had seen. Mr. Shadow told us he'd looked for a pink one all his life and had never seen one. So despite Steve's intense fuming, Jerry rerouted the trip *backward* so we could go retrieve the pink multiflora rose cuttings for Mr. Shadow and ourselves. Although they were unusual, they weren't anything to write home about unless they were going to be used for a rambling-rose breeding project. Unlike the white multiflora rootstock used in East Texas, they had thorns. They did, however, remind me of Ernest "Chinese" Wilson discovering and naming the pink-flowered *Rosa multiflora cathayensis* in China. I used to grow both of my Tennessee selections but destroyed them years ago. The last one I knew that existed was at the San Antonio Botanical Garden. Unfortunately, *Rosa multiflora* is invasive in the eastern United States and is the source of infection by the much-dreaded rose rosette disease.

"Laredo Cream Tea"

One tough hombre of a rose I recall came from the annual summer trip Dr. Parsons and I took to Laredo to search for colorful heat-tolerant plants. Jerry originally asked me to name the hottest place I could think of. I named a few, but he said HELL was the hottest place, and the closest thing to hell on earth was Laredo during the summertime! If a flower could bloom and tolerate a Laredo summer, it could tolerate anyplace in Texas. These summer trips to Laredo were where firebush (*Hamelia patens*) and esperanza (*Tecoma stans*) got their starts in the nursery industry and Texas gardens.

I remember making Jerry stop at a scruffy lawn mower repair shop where I spotted a large rose next to the front door. It was pretty apparent that they weren't

This tough tea rose survived in a neglected landscape in blistering Laredo, Texas.

very good at repairing mowers, because the unmowed lawn was strewn with broken ones! The cream-colored rose turned out to be an unknown true tea rose (*Rosa × odorata*). Teas are more normally associated with the humid Deep South but are obviously tough enough to tolerate even parched San Antonio and Laredo. I remember sitting in the hotel room that night watching the evening national news, during which the weatherman gave out the hottest temperature in the nation that day as Laredo's 107 degrees. I dubbed the rose "Laredo Cream Tea" and shared it with a number of Texas rose rustlers. I also planted it in several of my San Antonio rose collections, which have all unfortunately been destroyed. I regret that I don't have the rose anymore. With less than insane temperatures the flowers were actually peach colored.

'Speedy Gonzales'

One of the popular roses when I worked at the Antique Rose Emporium was "Martha Gonzales." It was a dwarfish red China rose found at the Navasota home of Martha Gonzales by Pam Puryear. Old books and descriptions seem to indicate that it was similar to (if not the same as) the 1832 cultivar 'Fabvier.' While I was working as the county horticulturist in San Antonio, Dr.

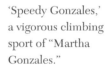

'Speedy Gonzales,' a vigorous climbing sport of "Martha Gonzales."

Parsons asked me to choose three useful antique roses that we could introduce to the nursery trade and home gardeners there. I chose 'Marie Pavié,'
"Caldwell Pink," and "Martha Gonzales." Because Peterson Brothers Nursery
sold them in four-inch pots, the three of them ended up being planted en
masse as landscape plants in a number of settings, including the Methodist
Hospital where Dr. Parsons was staying when he had a life-threatening bout
with Crohn's disease. I was told that he was in such bad shape that he might
not survive and that I should go see him immediately. As I headed through
the parking lot planted with "Martha Gonzales" roses, I couldn't help but
notice that one had produced a vigorous climbing sport. If Dr. Parsons had
taught me anything, it was to secure unusual plants without delay because
you might not have another opportunity. So, knowing that he might be dead
by the time I got to the room, I proceeded to take my climbing "Martha
Gonzales" rose cuttings first! I later named it 'Speedy Gonzales.' Although it's
not a common or popular rose, it is noted for its profusion of maroon foliage
ahead of bright red semidouble flowers. It has always served as a reminder to
me that the original China rose in the wild was a climber. I marvel at the fact
that all our double-flowered, ever-blooming shrub roses started out with *Rosa
chinensis spontanea*, a single-
flowered, once-blooming
climber. Interestingly enough,
I also found a climbing sport
of "Caldwell Pink" in a public
landscape planting near my
home in downtown San Antonio. I don't know whether
it's a blessing or a curse, but
I've always been gifted with
the ability to see the unusual
while overlooking the mun-
dane.

'Climbing Caldwell Pink'

When I first got to know Pam
Puryear and began visit-
ing her at her old home in

'Climbing
Caldwell Pink' is
a vigorous once-
blooming sport of
"Caldwell Pink."

THE YELLOW ROSE OF TEXAS   *Greg Grant*

Dr. Parsons lived through his hospital stay and went on to initiate his "Search for the Yellow Rose of Texas." Though he's not a native Texan, Jerry loves yellow roses—particularly those with a classic hybrid tea shape. My instructions were to look for any yellow roses performing well in a low-maintenance garden setting and propagate them for him to trial. As I drove to work each day, I couldn't help but notice a spectacular yellow rose underneath the porch overhang at the decrepit Stone Fort Motel in Nacogdoches. The motel had long since gone out of business and had individual families living in the rooms. Somebody was obviously into gardening, as the entire front of the run-down building was covered with both container and bedding plants. The next time Jerry was in town to visit me we secured cuttings from the yellow rose for his trial.

The story only gets thicker from here. We didn't have a study name for the rose so he just wrote "Nacogdoches" on the tag when he stuck them. When his volunteers potted up the plants they assumed that was its name. Jerry scattered the plants around, with the main collection being located at the home of Tillie Jungman, Dr. Larry Stein's grandmother, in Castroville,

The "Nacogdoches" rose was propagated from the former Stone Fort Motel in Nacogdoches, Texas.

Texas. Dr. Stein is an outstanding horticulturist from Castroville who serves as the project leader in the Texas AgriLife Extension horticulture program at Texas A&M University. This was classic Dr. Parsons, who loves to find enthusiastic participants to help look after his trials. All he had to do was evaluate the randomized, replicated yellow rose trial periodically. As it turned out, all of the roses from the same plant in Nacogdoches looked marginal, except for one that proved outstanding. Although I'm sure this grandiflora-ish rose has a true name, Dr. Parsons was convinced that the plant that excelled in his trial was a sport and genetically different from the original. Therefore, all subsequent plants were propagated from this single plant in Castroville. After that, Jerry renamed the plant previously known as "Nacogdoches" to "Grandma's Yellow" in honor of the late Tillie's hard work and dedication to the project. Its identity can be a bit confusing at times, because in addition to "Nacogdoches" and "Grandma's Yellow," it can also be purchased in Texas as "The Yellow Rose of Texas." Although her name and past might be a bit of a mystery, there's no doubt that this thorny yellow rose with healthy foliage and a profusion of shapely flowers is a popular and proven performer in Texas.

In Texas this showy rose is sold as "Grandma's Yellow," "Nacogdoches," and "The Yellow Rose of Texas."

"Caldwell Pink"
(image courtesy of
Mike Shoup).

Navasota, she had a climbing rose growing on the back corner of her porch that was thought to be 'Dorothy Perkins.' As it happened, Miss Dorothy was the first rose I ever grew, and I could see that Pam's rose was an imposter by its dull green foliage. If I remember correctly, even the Antique Rose Emporium carried this rose misnamed for some time. It actually looked like a climbing version of "Caldwell Pink." I later confirmed this when I noticed a climbing sport on a "Caldwell Pink" bush in a park not far from my King William District home in San Antonio. The occurrence of the climbing sport isn't rare, as I later saw it in downtown Nacogdoches and most recently at the San Antonio Botanical Garden. Like most climbing sports of ever-blooming shrubs, it's a spring bloomer only, but just as tough and beautiful.

'Farmer's Dream'

The most recent rose I rustled up was a climbing sport as well. In October 2012, Dr. Welch and I spoke at the Celebration of Roses in Farmers Branch, Texas. While there, I paid my first visit to their beautiful rose garden. Thanks to garden curator Pam Smith, the garden was in full bloom and beautiful shape. It included not only trial plants, but also a collection of those designated as Earth-Kind® roses by Texas AgriLife Extension. In the far corner of the garden I couldn't help but notice long, running canes coming from a 'Belinda's Dream' shrub. My first thought was that it was a rootstock suckering from below. But I quickly reminded myself that 'Belinda's Dream' is almost always grown on its own roots, and I recognized its distinct 'Belinda's Dream' foliage. I told Pam about it and asked her whether she wanted to propagate it or whether I could. She told me to do it and I told her I'd give the Farmers Branch rose garden credit by naming it 'Farmer's Dream.'

'Belinda's Dream' is one of the most popular roses in Texas, tabbed as both an Earth-Kind® selection and a Texas Superstar® by AgriLife Extension. It too was bred in Caldwell, Texas, by the late Dr. Robert Basye. When I became the county horticulturist in San Antonio, I secured cuttings of his 'Belinda's Dream' and sold plants through a program with the San Antonio Rose Society. I think they were the first 'Belinda's Dream' roses ever sold in the world.

I've grown the climbing form of 'Belinda's Dream' for only a few years now, but here's what I know. It's a very vigorous climber with strong canes about twelve feet

long. It's very easy to root from cuttings. It doesn't bloom the first year when it's producing its long shoots, and it appears to be primarily a spring bloomer somewhat like 'Climbing Old Blush.' I wondered whether it would repeat, as it's not uncommon for ever-blooming shrubs to sport once-blooming climbers, and vice versa. Like 'Belinda's Dream,' the extremely double flowers can

'Farmer's Dream,' a vigorous once-blooming sport of 'Belinda's Dream' (image courtesy of Ralph Anderson).

ball when it's humid and it gets some black spot on its foliage, which it sheds and replaces. The flowers have the same pleasant fragrance as her parent's, too. Everything about the plant is just like 'Belinda's Dream' except it makes long canes. I have it planted on both sides of my fence in my front garden.

"Pete Monzingo Rose"

The last rose I'll mention wasn't rustled by me, or by Bill. It was given to Bill in 1998, and he passed it on to me in 1999 along with this November 23 note that I recently dug from my long-stored files.

Pete Monzingo's Rose
Dr. William C. Welch, Extension Landscape Horticulturist

This rose was rescued from the 1998 flood in Del Rio by David and Becky Segrest after losing their home and its contents. According to Becky Segrest "Father had found the rose at the house he bought in

The pass-along "Monzingo Rose" from Del Rio, Texas.

1962. He was county agent in Val Verde County and always interested in plants as well as animals. He graduated from Texas A&M class of 1941. Pete used to supply his wife, Evelyn, with many fragrant bouquets of this rose as well as many other friends in Del Rio.

Becky Segrest brought plants to me immediately following the 1998 flood. They were in buckets of mud and the weather was hot. With help from Garry McDonald at the Texas A&M Horticulture Field Lab, the plants revived and a few cuttings were rooted. The plant is almost thornless, blooms repeatedly and has a nice fragrance. It has displayed excellent disease resistance during the time I have grown it. The color is a rich coral with a yellow flush near the base of the petals. Dr. and Mrs. Segrest live in the Bryan-College Station community.

The story doesn't end there, for I passed it on to my friend Greg Smith in Clear Lake, where we planted it at his new home along with a collection of other rustled antique roses I had on hand. It turns out that like my friend Dr. Jerry Parsons, Greg Smith likes the look of modern roses, not smaller-flowered antique ones, so when he moved to Friendswood, the only rose he took with him was the "Pete Monzingo Rose." While passing through in 2014 to pick up some rolls of double-loop wire fencing nearby, I stopped and took cuttings from it. I knew it was from Del Rio, but for all these years I thought it was one that I had collected from a home there while I was the county horticulturist in San Antonio. It wasn't until I found this note from Bill that I realized I had lost my Del Rio rose but saved his! After all this, I figured it had earned the right to be in my little cottage garden, so there the "Monzingo Rose" lives on. Thank you, Pete, Becky, Bill, and friend Greg. This is a happy ending to the common plight of once being lost, but now being found.

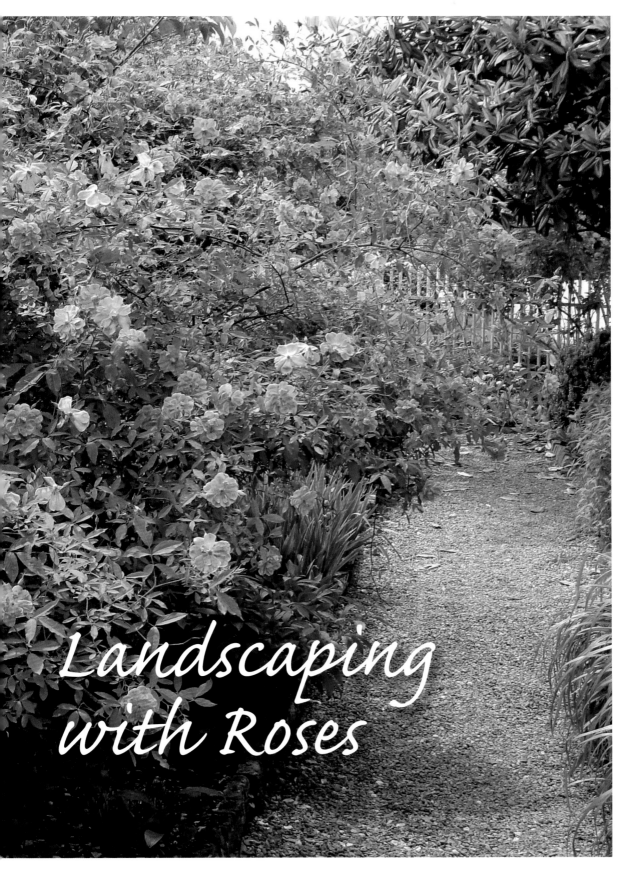

Landscaping with Roses

GREG'S GARDENS

I can thank Bill Welch, Mike Shoup, and the Antique Rose Emporium for opening my eyes to landscaping with roses. Remember, I was born in Tyler, Texas, famous for producing field-grown hybrid tea roses, and was taught in college that these finicky modern developments belonged in a bed by themselves, hidden from view in the backyard where they could be sprayed, pruned, and coddled into glorious long-stemmed bloom. Fortunately, falling into Bill's hands at Texas A&M and working with him and Mike in graduate school at the soon to be opened Antique Rose Emporium gave me a much-needed crash course in landscaping with many different kinds of heirloom roses, all much more adapted and suited for landscaping than the single class of modern hybrid teas I had dealt with previously.

But I was still an inquisitive young horticulturist and was interested in trialing individual plants, not artistic landscaping. Bill helped me pick out an introductory list of roses to grow from the fascinating new Antique Rose Emporium catalog. Oh, how I loved perusing those tempting early descrip-

Greg's first collection of young mail-order antique roses from the Antique Rose Emporium.

tions and accompanying pictures. I planted the tiny things in a row along a fence at my parents' new ranch house in rural East Texas. Thanks to Pam Puryear and her very active Texas Rose Rustlers, I was hooked on hunting long-abandoned roses, and thanks to a fresh degree in horticulture, I was hooked on trialing and growing these roses side by side to see which were more adapted and what growth habits they formed. One fencerow grew into another fencerow, and another, and another—eventually peaking at 84 different kinds of found roses at my parents' ranch. This was in addition to placing other trial rose plantings and collections with willing cooperators associated with my work as the county horticulturist for the Texas Agricultural Extension Service in San Antonio. I sincerely regret that I no longer have many of those found roses and often wonder whether any of those cooperators kept any of them. I am saddened to know that the old Bexar County courthouse and the San Antonio Botanical Garden removed theirs. Those were my children!

My first real attempt at landscaping with these new-to-me old roses occurred at a good friend's new home in Victoria, Texas. Another lesson for budding young horticulturists: you will be expected to provide free design, free advice, free plants, and free labor to make sure all of your friends, relatives, and neighbors have pretty landscapes too. Since my friend lived in a Victorian-style new home in the town of Victoria, I thought a vintage rose landscape seemed very appropriate. I propagated a host of rosy children and hauled them his way. Certainly we couldn't plant a thing until we hand-dug the St. Augustinegrass sod from the beds, and first I had to recover from a broken eye socket gained from running full speed into a mailbox while playing football in the street in front of his house. And folks wonder why I've had eight bone and spine surgeries.

The eventual results turned out quite nice, featuring masses of 'Marie Pavié' polyantha roses in front of the porch, a 'Mrs. Dudley Cross' tea rose specimen on the porch corner, a sweep of Gulf muhly grass (*Muhlenbergia capillaris*) to the right of the sidewalk, and the entire curvilinear beds bordered by low-trimmed "Martha Gonzales" China roses, similar to an English garden lined with Dutch boxwood. When my friend sold this house, moved to another, and asked for yet another free landscape, I quickly implemented a new policy of a single "get out of landscaping" card for each friend and relative.

With a little more confidence behind me, my next attempt at landscaping came again at my parents' ranch. By then I had decided that their home would certainly look better with more suitable landscaping instead of row

Greg's design
and installation
handiwork in a
Victoria, Texas,
landscape.

after row of trial plants. The trial roses were removed. The first landscape roses I planted on the property were masses of the thornless memorial rose (*Rosa wichuraiana inermis*) on either side of the entrance next to the highway. It was a nod to several nearby remaining stands of its later offspring 'Dorothy Perkins,' and also a low-maintenance ground-cover choice for an area that would receive no irrigation and minimal attention. The stand lasted for a decade or so, until the highway department started mowing it down twice a year. And without any proof, I also began to worry about the possibility of it becoming invasive like its Asian cousin *Rosa multiflora*.

I had also planted a personal favorite, the delicately beautiful and intensely fragrant 'Marie Pavié,' around my mom's patio so others could enjoy her attributes. Then one season I happened to notice a branch with pinker flowers on it. 'Marie Pavié' typically has soft pink buds that open into white flowers. This new branch sport (an accidental appearance of something different on a plant) had bright pink buds and medium to soft pink flowers. I took cuttings of it, rooted them, and found them to be stable. I named it for a dear old lady whose yard I mowed as a kid growing up in Longview. Although

I was told she was a "witch," Marie Daly turned out to be one of the sweetest, most loving people I ever met. She loved flowers and loved me, and I in turn loved her.

I established a new bed of 'Marie Daly' next to the driveway parking area so I could evaluate it and have cutting stock for propagation purposes. For some reason that I can't recall, I removed the original bed of 'Marie Pavié' and replaced it with dwarf yaupon and assorted pink and white perennials. We garden designers are always painting new pictures. When I later abandoned my poor mother's landscape entirely and succumbed to my dad's initial complaints that he couldn't back his truck up to the back patio to unload his firewood, I removed the new bed of 'Marie Daly' and took the freshly dug, bare-root plants down to my own garden. They were my children, after all. I grow a small hedge of 'Marie Daly' in my back garden so she can stay with me as long as I live. We both loved birds, so I make sure a bluebird nest box and the black oil sunflower feeder are nearby.

The long-lost highlight of my parents' hilltop country landscape was a

'Marie Pavié' on the left and her pinker sport 'Marie Daly' on the right.

210-foot perennial border I planted across the front of the property. After learning about Southern-adapted perennials from Dr. Welch, visiting fine European borders, and listening to others who persisted in saying "perennials won't grow in the South," I took on this massive project to provide a showy example and prove otherwise. I dubbed it "The Rainbow Border," as it was basically a linear color wheel, starting with red flowers on the left and working its way through purple, blue, green, yellow, orange, and finally red again on the far right. It was one of the finest creations of my life. It was actually a mixed border, as I included appropriately colored shrubs as well, including three specimens of what I still think was 'Cramoisi Superieur' collected from a garden south of San Antonio in the left red section, a green rose (*Rosa chinensis* 'Viridiflora') in the green section, and what Bill said was 'Climbing Cramoisi Superieur' along the fence in the far right red section. It proved to be a bush form and matched those on the left side. Unfortunately, as my former herculean self declined, the yard became overrun with grandchildren, and my mother's age caught up with her, I removed the border so my newly retired father could maintain the front with a hay mower, finishing mower, and riding lawn mower. He's a tractor man. I try not to think about my beautiful lost border.

The far right side of Greg's "Rainbow Border" featured Texas-tough yellow, orange, and red pass-along perennials.

Today the Grant Ranch landscape features a restored log corncrib and a few of Greg's rustled roses (image courtesy of Ralph Anderson).

With my dad now in charge of mowing, I was also forced to remove the two "Fanick's Pink Marechal Niel" roses I had planted on their restored square-notched log corncrib. It turns out he doesn't like "bushes," especially thorny ones. The landscape that once boasted around one hundred roses now claims only four mystery red Chinas, a 'Belinda's Dream,' a 'Ducher,' and a "Satin Cream Tea." To each his own.

I was not to be without roses myself, however. It wasn't long before I tackled a nearby family house restoration project in a little ancestral hamlet. It was the very house, just down the road from my parents, where my great-grand-mother "Big Momma" lived most of her life. After the death of Big Momma's daughter, my great-aunt Ruby Dee Smith, who had lived there for years as well, my dad purchased the property along with what had once been his grand-parents' old dogtrot farmhouse.

I spent a year cleaning it out and opening the porches and dogtrot back up. My good friend and master carpenter Larry Shelton then spent another year restoring it to its near-original condition. My very first order of business was to return to the landscape the three roses that Big Momma used to grow. Luckily for me, I had earlier propagated these horticultural family heirlooms, as my good friend Ruby Dee wasn't a gardener, and along with her large animal menagerie, she gradually killed the originals off. I didn't own the home and knew I wouldn't be there permanently, so I knew I should strategically place any ornamental plantings to ensure their chance of survival. One way to do that was to line them up with other plants and structures so that the hired

All of Greg's great-grandmother's surviving roses were planted in a row at her restored dogtrot house, with "Big Momma's Blush" to the left and a young plant of her white-flowered "Big Momma's Musk" to the right (image courtesy of Ralph Anderson).

mowers didn't have to go out of their way to mow around them. We all know how that turns out.

I placed two "Big Momma's Blush" tea roses out in front to frame the dogtrot breezeway as one viewed it from the highway or entered the front gate. Their location wasn't far from the original roses or the offspring clone that I knew growing up. I also placed two of her "Big Momma's Musk" roses in the same line, but farther out so as to frame the house itself. These were all in line with three existing old pink crapemyrtles (*Lagerstroemia indica*). And far to the right I planted one of her "Maggie" roses so that all were in the same line and whoever was mowing wouldn't have to deviate much for any of them. The whole line is parallel to both the double-loop wire fence out front and the housefront itself. It made me feel good that all of her roses were planted near the originals, too.

I went on to plant two of my favorite antique roses in line with the back windows and parallel to an existing double lavender althea (*Hibiscus syriacus*) on the left and one of Big Momma's surviving cape jasmines (*Gardenia jasminoides*) on the right. This way, when I looked out what was now the bathroom window (the house wasn't built with an indoor bathroom), I'd be looking at my beloved pink 'Duchesse de Brabant,' and when I looked directly out the north kitchen window, I'd lay eyes on the real 'Louis Philippe' rose originally shared by late friend and Texas Rose Rustler Pam Puryear. This rose was his-

'Duchesse de Brabant' is planted near a window at Big Momma's dogtrot so it can be seen and smelled (image courtesy of Ralph Anderson).

torically known as the "Creole rose" in Louisiana and as the "cracker rose" in Florida. If I had remained living there, I would have planted rambling roses on all four corners of the fence, but since I wouldn't be there to train and weed around them, I decided against it. I lived there for several years while Larry was restoring my grandparents' dogtrot house just down the road.

From Big Momma's I moved back into what I call the Emanis House—one that I actually own. For most of my life it belonged to my maternal grandparents, Eloy and Marquette Emanis. Long before that, it once belonged to my Grandmother Emanis's grandparents, Bob and Mary Pate, who lived there with a houseful of children and ran the country store out front. The house was built as a dogtrot, with an open breezeway or "dog run" through the middle of it, which was closed in by my great-aunt and uncle, Nara and Voyd Hughes, after Arcadia got electricity in 1949. Nara was my Papaw's older sister. I'll be the first to admit that the landscape around my old restored family home is no rose wonderland. First of all, I'm trying to stay true to my poor, spartan family roots, not known for frivolous nonedible plants or artistic landscape expression. But of course I can't help myself and squeeze in heat- and drought-tolerant ornamentals that can be mowed around with a tractor and survive the occasional mobile drunken relative or livestock stampede. I use mostly period-appropriate heirlooms and plants that I've introduced to the

nursery trade. The most noticeable landscape feature is an allée of purplish crapemyrtles leading up to the house. I propagated this cold-hardy heirloom selection from the old Thelma and Ezra Wheeler home place nearby and call it the Arcadia crapemyrtle or "Thelma Wheeler."

Bottom line, my little rose garden is actually a hodgepodge collection that serves as a multipurpose chicken yard, fruit orchard, and crinum collection. It's tough being a plant collector, nurseryman, farmer, and landscaper! My little rose garden currently consists of individual specimens of 'Mrs. B. R. Cant,' 'Mrs. Dudley Cross,' 'Violette,' "Scottsville Gallica," "Satin Cream Tea," and "Bryan Fredel Tea." I do use the henhouse (my grandmother's old car shed) for climbers, as they lend themselves quite well to less-than-formal old farmstead landscapes. There's a nice old multitrunked female yaupon holly (*Ilex vomitoria*) on the east side of the structure, which leaves three corners open for the softening effect of climbing roses. On the back corners, inside the chicken yard, I have my old San Antonio buddies, "Fanick's

An heirloom indica crapemyrtle rooted from cuttings Greg took at an old home place nearby forms an allée in front of the Emanis House.

Pink Marechal Niel" and the "Flores Street House Eater Rose." And on the exposed front north corner, where my Granny and I once grew our rustled 'Dorothy Perkins,' I have a beautiful specimen of the hot-pink thornless rambler I call "Queenie."

I once had two 'Farmer's Dream' (Climbing Belinda's Dream) roses on a specially made arbor over the chicken yard entrance gate but decided her long, vigorous canes would make a better show on my front cottage garden fence, so I removed them and replaced them with "Pam's Pink" honeysuckle (*Lonicera* × *americana*). The little cottage garden in front of my house is only twenty by forty feet and is enclosed with double-loop wire fencing, with my old white frame house as a backdrop. The garden inside the fence is composed of drifts of vigorous perennials in various shades of pink, blue, and purple, including John Fanick phlox (*Phlox paniculata* 'John Fanick'), Pam Puryear Turk's cap (*Malvaviscus drummondii* 'Pam Puryear'), Henry Duelberg salvia (*Salvia farinacea* 'Henry Duelberg'), Little Boy Blue salvia

Greg once grew both "Peggy Martin" (left) and "Queenie" (right) on the front of his henhouse.

(*Salvia azurea* 'Little Boy Blue'), Peppermint Flare rose mallow (*Hibiscus moscheutos* 'Peppermint Flare'), and Jackie Grant rose mallow (*Hibiscus* × 'Jackie Grant'). It's bisected through the middle by a brick path leading to the front steps. The antique bricks came from my Granny Ruth's old dilapidated chimney. Each side of the garden is punctuated in its center with tall, bold specimens of the old French hybrid *Canna* × *iridiflora* 'Ehemannii,' which looks like a cross between a banana and a fuchsia. The back edge, under the drip line of the tin roof, is anchored by a row of my Grandmother Emanis's favorite *Crinum* × 'Ellen Bosanquet.' The outside of the fence is thickly bordered by locally collected Byzantine gladiolus (*Gladiolus byzantinus*) with a climbing 'Belinda's Dream' rose (*Rosa* × 'Farmer's Dream') on each side to help frame a close view of the house. These are the same spots where I formerly grew 'Pam's Pink' honeysuckles. The four-foot-high space on the fence will give the vigorous rose canes more room to spread out and ultimately provide more of a show than the chicken yard arbor did. It looks like Climbing Belinda's Dream will be primarily a spring bloomer, like other climbing sports of ever-blooming shrub roses. That's quite all right, though, as there are many summer- and fall-blooming perennials nearby, along with two old pink crapemyrtles propagated from my Emanis great-grandparents' old home place not far away, providing the ultimate frame for the house. I recently added two "Monzingo" roses to the back corners, next to the outside corners of the porch. It didn't take me long, however, to decide that Mr. Monzingo should go in my proposed new rose garden behind the house, so I replaced them with the new dark purple, dwarf 'Purple Magic' crapemyrtles that I will cut to the ground each year and grow as "herbaceous" perennials.

My Papaw's old lean-to car shed is attached to the left of the house and required a bit of softening, so I grow Dr. Basye's single, thornless *Rosa bank-*

The front cottage garden at the Emanis House features color-themed heat-tolerant perennials.

Dr. Basye's single-flowered 'Fragrant Snowflake' perfumes the entire property at the Emanis House.

siae 'Fragrant Snowflake' there and train its vigorous canes over the front edge, beneath the tin roof. I drive under it to park each day and in the spring-time the mass of tiny delicate white flowers scent the entire garden. However, now that the pink crapemyrtles are blocking (and shading) the front of the car shed, I'm considering moving 'Fragrant Snowflake' to an open area where I can grow it as a huge shrub.

On the outside of this less-than-attractive lean-to car shed, I grow the thornless, once-blooming, pink and white rambler thousand beauties (*Rosa multiflora* 'Tausendschon'). Though some reject once-blooming roses, I certainly don't. After all, who doesn't find useful beauty in dogwoods, mountain laurels, redbuds, spireas, and other showy, once-blooming plants? And when the showy multicolored clusters of 'Tausendschon' are in bloom, everybody wants one!

Behind the car shed, just outside my crown tire parterre kitchen garden I have a small border featuring peony poppies and bunny bloom larkspur during the spring, and later, white Duelberg sage (*Salvia farinacea* 'Augusta Duelberg') around a specimen of my single-flowered Martha Turnbull hip gardenia (*Gardenia jasminoides* 'Martha Turnbull'). My plans are to replace the hip gardenia with a large-growing chinquapin rose and put the gardenias

Greg still grows
the thousand
beauties rose
he rescued as a
cutting at Texas
A&M years ago.

on the side of the henhouse, where I removed three oakleaf hydrangeas that
I was tired of watering each summer. I usually plant the side of the border
next to my Granny's large old Celeste fig with cutting stock of my variegated
Pentas lanceolata 'Stars and Stripes' during the summer. I'm gradually adding
more pink and white perennials to this area. On the back side of this small
triangular border I have a nice hedge of my Marie Daly rose (*Rosa polyantha*
'Marie Daly'). It does a fine job of providing a bit of enclosure to the area
along with scenting the entire space when in bloom. These are the plants I
rescued from my parents' place when they were getting out of the gardening
business.

The one other rose on the property is my climbing sport of "Martha Gonzales" (*Rosa chinensis* 'Speedy Gonzales'), which I grow on the barbed-wire
fence behind the brick Masonic Lodge out front. It's the ugliest structure in
Arcadia. I wish 'Speedy' would cover the entire thing!

By the time you read this I hope to have created a new rose garden
immediately behind my old dogtrot house in Arcadia. For years I've had
a crown tire kitchen parterre garden there, but now that I've sold my last
crop of Byzantine gladiolus I will grow most of my vegetables in my large
fenced-in garden next to the house. I've always kept a swept yard between
the tire planters but have had some problems with erosion, mud, and porch

footprints. After planting the roses I'll mulch the entire area with homegrown pine straw to help alleviate this problem. I will keep my two blueberry plants but will move my asparagus from the five tire planters into one long row in the vegetable garden. I've always dreamed of a long row of delicious asparagus. I originally collected this asparagus from a pasture on the old Darnell Place where my parents built their home. I don't know what cultivar it is, but I assume John and Fannie Matt Darnell along with their sons Travis and Russell dined on it. Travis and Russell were childhood pals and neighbors of my Granny Ruth.

I will add one raised bed in my new rose garden for special vegetables like salad greens, herbs, and Dr. Parson's trial tomatoes each year. I'll also keep my little brick bed for summer zinnias and winter cabbage. Otherwise, the rest will be mostly roses and pine straw. I'm planning on a hedge of 'Cecile Brunner' along the double-loop wire fence, punctuated by a large new arbor to support my gargantuan Climbing Belinda's Dream ('Farmer's Dream') rose. I've now decided the front fence isn't large enough for it. I will

A small hedge of Greg's 'Marie Daly' rose defines the back edge of his Emanis House garden.

Greg got his start of asparagus from that surviving at an old home place in the community.

have a smaller arbor at the end of my little 'Marie Daly' hedge where I'll put my old favorite 'Veilchenblau.' I also plan to use several 'Enchantress' tea roses against the back of the house, and next to the porch I'd like to grow a specimen of 'LaMarne.' I will line up two "Monzingo" roses with the blueberries to frame the back view of my dogtrot porch and put one specimen of my "Satin Cream Tea" back there to use for breeding purposes. My house faces east so I can't wait to peer across my rose garden and see the sunrise through my breezeway. Nothing makes me happier than painting a rosy picture in my head and then planting it.

BILL'S GARDENS

Rehburg Garden

The best learning experiences of my career have been my personal gardens. Each garden location presented different challenges in terms of soil, existing hardscape, and style of structures. My interest in period garden design grew over the years undeterred by these challenges, and certain universal truths regarding landscaping with roses became apparent. For example, features such as fences, pergolas, and walks are very important to showcase certain roses, especially climbing roses, which shine in new and old gardens. The versatility of old roses as small as 'Marie Pavié' and "Highway 290 Pink Buttons" and as large as Lady Banks offers opportunities to clothe gardens as small as patio homes or as large as ranch or plantation homes, where climbers can be allowed to clamber over walls, fences, and sheds. Of course, I developed personal preferences along the way, as well. I have always preferred a palette of soft colors: pink, purple, white, blush, rose, and violet. Although I enjoy

Front elevation prior to garden installation.

After planting.

Stone path and
front planting.

Another view of the front garden.

red and orange in the gardens of others, I rarely have them in mine. Here, I describe the various gardens I have designed and tended and the valuable lessons they have provided and continue to provide. I declare all of them to be labors of a rosarian's love.

Rehburg was my first "country garden." It was located on twenty-seven acres in Washington County with a small turn-of-the-last-century farmhouse amid cedars (*Juniperus virginiana*). The soil was relatively poor and alkaline and the only water was from the well that served the house, so my plant choices needed to be tough and drought resistant. It was here that I experimented with the first old roses I found and bought. The roses from this garden were among the first selected for the foundation stock at the Antique Rose Emporium. I supplemented the roses at Rehburg with named varieties from Roses of Yesterday and Today in California and gifts from Dr. Robert Basye.

The wooden gate and woven wire fence provided an appropriate entrance and enclosure to the front garden. The native stone walk was in place but was covered by a couple of inches of soil that had accumulated over the years. I arranged roses and perennials that I had grown from cuttings in a four- to five-foot-wide planting bed that spanned about seventy-five feet. The planting started under an existing cedar tree and ended under a nice specimen of Mexican plum (*Prunus mexicana*) that was already there. Photographs

The front gate at the Rehburg garden, showing the beginnings of my historical rose collection.

of the gate planting appeared as the cover of the first catalog of the Antique Rose Emporium. The next year's cover featured cut roses from the Rehburg garden in an antique stoneware pitcher displayed on the front porch of the house.

Perennials like the German red carnation, oxeye daisy (*Chrysanthemum leucanthemum*), and cemetery white iris (*Iris × albicans*) were present along with bachelor buttons (*Gomphrena globosa*), Johnny-jump-ups (*Viola* spp.) and old-fashioned petunias that reseeded on their own each year along with larkspurs and poppies. Typically when gardens were created during the late 1800s, families and neighbors traded plants and few were purchased.

This garden served as a destination for one of the first Rose Rustles. My late wife, Diane, and I created it in the early 1980s. The restoration of the house was done mainly by us. My son, Will, reminds me that he helped paint the exterior. When we purchased it the house had been abandoned for about ten years. It was small (about 1,200 square feet), but the rooms and ceilings were large and the front porch was eight feet wide and extended across the entire front of the house. Outside were a few peach, plum, and apricot trees.

Cricket Court

Our second effort at creating a country garden was very different from that on the Rehburg property. We named the place for the masses of crickets we encountered when we first visited there. The house was High Victorian, with nice trim work and a beautiful bay window in the living room. The front of the house opened onto an open lawn that extended about one hundred feet to where it terminated in a grove of old live oaks.

Nancy Volkman, ASLA, was a friend and member of the landscape architecture faculty at Texas A&M, where she was recognized for her knowledge of garden and architectural history. I asked for her assistance with some ideas to create an appropriate garden.

We decided to create a courtyard on each end of the house. The larger one

Garden arch covered with 'Veilchenblau' rose.

was about forty by sixty feet and terminated with a raised gazebo covered with 'Climbing Cecile Brunner' and 'Trier' rambler roses. The courtyard space was formally arranged with granite gravel walks and an antique cast-iron urn in the center. Arched gates framed both sides and were covered with 'Veilchenblau' (violet/purple) roses. 'Zephirine Drouhin,' 'Marechal Niel,' and blackberry roses were trained on the picket fences that were constructed

'Marechal Niel' rose trained on fence.

'Trier Rambler' and 'Climbing Cecile Brunner' cover gazebo.

of cypress lumber harvested from our farm in Louisiana. Dr. Basye had grafted 'Marechal Niel' onto one of his *R.* × *fortuniana* rootstocks to provide it with more vigor. For many years, this rose was considered the most beautiful climbing rose of all. Its lack of cold hardiness restricted its use to the Deep South. The soil was fairly heavy clay and I added large volumes of composted pine bark to amend the beds.

Other roses in the main courtyard were 'Sombreuil,' which was espaliered on the fence, and "Katy Road Pink" ('Carefree Beauty'), which was massed on both sides of the walk in front of the gazebo. The dark pink flowers, almost continuous bloom, outstanding fragrance, and disease resistance of the latter make

Antique urn at center of herb garden.

"Cricket Court" before garden.

Perennial borders filled in quickly with old-fashioned plants well adapted to these surroundings.

Oxeye daisies and German red carnations combined with 'Old Blush' roses at the fence line.

it one of my all-time favorites. 'Sombreuil' has outstanding fragrance as well, and its highly formal, many-petaled, creamy white flowers are among the most beautiful of all roses.

We created a curving walk from the gate across the front of the house connecting to another gate that entered the second courtyard, which was planted primarily with herbs. The two entry gates from the front walk into the courtyards had arched coverings that repeated the angle of the gables on the house.

Dr. Robert Basye gave me several hundred two-inch clay pots that I used as edging for the oval center and sides of the herb garden, which also had an antique urn as its focal point. I had noted this idea for edging in Ryan Gainey's beautiful Atlanta garden. Dr. Basye also provided a fortuniana rose. We installed a sprinkler system, which helped to establish the newly set-out plants and get us through extended dry spells.

The house at Cricket Court was built in nearby Carmine, Texas, in the 1890s. It was moved to its current site in Washington County in the 1970s. There was an abandoned water well that gave me the idea to find an old windmill. My friend Mrs. Faith Bybee collected old houses in the Round Top area, and a particularly beautiful home in nearby Warrenton had a tall windmill close by. Mrs. Bybee was glad to give up the windmill since it really wasn't appropriate to the period of her house, and she happily traded it for

A close-up of 'Zephirine Drouhin,' 1868.

antique roses for her project at Henkel Square in Round Top. It had also been overgrown by a vigorous live oak. I loved having the additional water source, along with the pleasant sounds of the windmill. I was also overjoyed that the base of each of the four windmill legs provided a great place to plant more antique roses.

Fragilee

Several years after we sold Cricket Court, I decided that I wanted to restore an early Texas house and create an appropriate garden surrounding it. Our friends the Ponders had purchased some property adjacent to their ranch near Burton, and there was a very old, dilapidated home there. After looking it over, we determined that it was indeed an old structure, probably from the 1850s. The Ponders didn't want it and said we could have it if we would move it off its current site. They offered to sell us four acres on a corner of their land if we wanted to restore it there. My first thought was to move it to Round Top, where Mrs. Bybee had sold me a two-acre tract in town hoping that I would establish a nursery featuring old roses and other heirloom plants for the growing number of Houston families who were restoring homes and building new ones in the area.

It was a difficult decision, but we decided to accept the Ponders' offer and keep the house in the country. The site we had purchased was open prairie with no trees. The views were beautiful and we selected a high spot adjacent to an existing metal barn and shed.

I asked Yoakum House Movers to take a look at the house and determine whether it was sturdy enough to withstand the stress of the move. Mr. Yoakum looked the house over carefully and responded, "The house is very fragile, but I think it will withstand the move if we ask the termites to hold hands." During the moving process the house was fine, but the front porch did fall off.

With the help of a good craftsperson and some research, we discovered that the structure was actually two one-room houses that were joined with a connecting hall and stairway leading to the sleeping lofts over the rooms. We kept it as we found it and developed the upstairs sleeping lofts into two bedrooms and a bath in the hall space. The original downstairs porch was enlarged to eight feet wide. We loved the experience of restoring an early Texas home and were anxious to accept the challenge of creating an appropriate garden. We knew the garden needed to be simple and relatively small. I was determined to feature old roses and other heirloom plants available to Texas gardeners in the mid to late 1800s.

The house sat pretty high, and the ground elevation of the front side was a couple of feet higher than that of the rear. This gave us an opportunity to design a broad and impressive stairway from the front porch to the front lawn. It also provided space to include six-foot-wide beds across the front that I filled with 'Old Blush' roses and a single large crapemyrtle on each corner. The views from the porch were impressive. The bluebonnets and other wildflowers were stunning in spring. The picturesque manicured pastures and large stock pond over the fence on the Ponders' ranch and several miles beyond beckoned the eyes farther.

We decided to name the place Fragilee because it had been so fragile that it was almost unsalvageable. The back and side gardens were developed like the early swept gardens of our ancestors (no lawn). I chose to create a simple parterre in the back with a center and four radiating beds each anchored with a clipped pyramid of myrtle (*Myrtus communis*). Cynthia Mueller rooted the myrtle cuttings from Mrs. Ripper in Schulenburg, who had a wonderful cottage garden filled with roses and other heirlooms. The cuttings grew quickly and added a nice touch of formality. The center of the parterre featured five plants of "Martha Gonzales" roses flanking a small concrete obelisk. The bed was bordered with rain lilies.

A view through the arbor to the surrounding countryside.

"Martha Gonzales" roses surround an obelisk. The outer foliage is composed of 'Grandjax' rain lilies.

A twelve-by-eighteen-foot gazebo, crowned with an antique lead finial I found in Fredericksburg, provided support for a huge specimen of white Lady Banks rose that came from Elizabeth Lawrence's original plant in Charlotte, North Carolina. A rustic cedar table and chairs from Jason and Shelley Powell's Petals from the Past nursery were sheltered by the huge umbrella of rose foliage. An additional delight was the violet scent associated with the white Lady Banks rose. Cynthia Mueller had rooted the cuttings along with a climbing red China rose that Peggy Cornett (horticulturist at Monticello) had rustled from a Victorian garden in Williamsburg. The opposite corner of the gazebo had a specimen of 'Madame Alfred Carriere' that blooms many months of the year. In the early days, weddings were sometimes planned to coincide with the massive spring bloom. Three heirloom purple crapemyrtles were also grown from cuttings from a friend in Brenham.

We salvaged most of the original cypress siding on the house and stained it a weathered gray. We contrasted it with a maroon trim that was an exact color match with the burgundy castor bean plants that provided generous amounts of foliage each summer. Mounds of bachelor buttons (*Gomphrena*

Lady Banks, 'Old Blush,' and "Peggy Martin" roses dominate the plantings in the side garden.

Fall bounty from the gourd and pumpkin patches at Fragilee.

Specimen of 'Climbing Cramoisi Superieur' on a gate at Fragilee.

globosa) and old-fashioned reseeding petunias were also colorful and low-maintenance sources of winter, spring, and summer color. Greg introduced 'Laura Bush' petunias about that time as well, and they made themselves right at home at Fragilee.

Picket fences were constructed from cypress harvested at our farm near Mangham, Louisiana. I also designed arches that reflected the angles of the gables of the house. These were draped with old climbing roses such as 'Climbing Old Blush,' 'Madame Alfred Carriere,' and "Queenie," a thornless, once-blooming climbing rose I collected in Austin.

The side garden included the

air conditioning equipment that I attempted to screen with picket fencing. Peggy Martin gave me a cutting of the rambling rose from her lovely garden in Plaquemines Parish, Louisiana, that I first named "The Air Conditioner Rose" because I planted it on the fence to help screen the air conditioning equipment. Of course, I later named it "Peggy Martin."

In addition to old roses, I learned more about heirloom bulbs, peaches, and citrus at Fragilee. The wide openness of the site taught me about creating shade structures for roses and grape arbors that were similar to those used in early Texas gardens. I also learned more about gardening with less water and the value of organic materials in heavy, dry soils.

An eight-by-forty-foot grape arbor was added across the west-facing open side of a large metal barn. It was planted with 'Champanel' grapes, which were resistant to insects, disease, and drought and were created in the late 1800s by T. V. Munson of Denison, Texas. This helped me understand first-hand why Texas and Southern gardeners loved having vine-covered arbors to create cool, inviting retreats in our long, hot summers. Both roses and grapes were excellent choices for covering arbors and casting shade.

A view of the Mangham cottage from the front, showing the "Natchitoches Noisette" rose.

Mangham, Louisiana

Northeast Louisiana provides a different gardening experience from that in Central Texas. Although similar to Tyler and East Texas in general, there are

some differences. It is more like the rest of the Southeast, so I can relate well to friends who garden in those areas. Technically, our property is in USDA Hardiness Zone 8B. It is a bit colder and wetter, but more importantly, the soils are more acidic and nutrient rich. Azaleas and camellias thrive in Mangham, as do dogwoods, osmanthus, and many types of *Narcissus*. Roses also thrive in these conditions.

My late wife's family owned farm property and a 1900s-era home in the small town of Mangham (population seven hundred), which is about thirty miles southeast of Monroe. We maintain it as a family getaway. In this area, family cemeteries are well kept and often contain interesting historical plants. My first old rose discovery was "Maggie," still growing at another family homesite on the original farm. I also found the very rare double form of the swamp rose (*Rosa palustris scandens*) growing there.

To illustrate what a small world it is, a woman originally from Mangham introduced herself after a lecture at the old Hastings Nursery in Atlanta, Georgia. Recently, she said, she and her husband had visited my father-in-law in Mangham and discussed the "Maggie" rose. As they talked, my father-in-law's ranch dog Bob (the dog from hell) began leaping around seeking attention and broke off the main branch of the newly planted "Maggie" rose bush in the front yard. She asked whether she could take the cutting back with her to Atlanta and try to root it in her garden. After my program in Atlanta, we were invited to her home. I was delighted to see that the cutting was now a large bush and in full flower.

Later, we decided to renovate the house and plant a garden. There were beautiful old specimens of azaleas and camellias scattered about the site, as well as heirloom bulbs, large saucer magnolias, pecans, figs, sweet olive, banana shrubs, old-fashioned mop-head hydrangeas, several kinds of spirea, forsythia, and flowering almond (*Prunus glandulosa*). As time passed, storms and old age wreaked changes that opened some areas up to more sunlight. Jessie Lee Harris took an interest in helping us care for the place many years ago and is still involved with rustling many bulbs and other plants for the garden.

Early in my rose rustling career, I found "Natchitoches Noisette" growing in the American cemetery in Natchitoches, Louisiana. It was not adjacent to a headstone and I wasn't sure what to call it. After some study, there is still a question as to whether it is a Noisette rose, but its value as a landscape plant is undisputed. A large specimen greets visitors near the front door and there is another planted in the back garden inside a tire planter created by

"Peggy Martin" roses trained over the arches of the matching picket fence gates.

Greg Grant. The same day, I found "McClinton Tea" also growing in a Natchitoches neighborhood. Mrs. McClinton graciously shared cuttings of her lovely, fragrant tea rose. These two roses still stand out as favorites, even after many years.

The renovations in the garden included new cypress picket fences with matching gates framed by arches draped with large specimens of "Peggy Martin" roses. This is the same architectural feature I used at Cricket Court and Fragilee. I enjoy the repetition of familiar motifs in my gardens. I did the same thing with the ridge crest, a cut metal tulip and star design from an old Texas roof that was re-created by a metal craftsperson in Brenham, Texas, and that appeared first at Fragilee and later at Twin Oaks.

The original front and back walks consisted of a few stepping stones and uneven turf. The front porch is particularly nice, and I thought it should have a generous-sized antique brick walk and landing area for people to congregate and visit as they come and go from the house. Now the walks are four feet wide and direct traffic from the parking area and to the rear gate and entrance, where another brick landing area of similar size (eight by ten feet) serves the back door. Nearby are clusters of St. Joseph's lily (*Hippeastrum × johnsonii*) and 'Apple Blossom' amaryllis.

Among the features of this garden are drifts and edgings of lavender-pink prairie phlox (*Phlox pilosa*) originally from Ruth Knopf in South Carolina,

who obtained it from Elizabeth Lawrence, the famous garden writer from
Charlotte, North Carolina. Soon after I brought the first ones to Mangham,
Jessie Lee enthusiastically began increasing their number. Soon they were
everywhere in our garden. Jessie Lee bordered existing flower beds and
massed them with bulbs. Within a couple of years, our phlox appeared in just
about every garden on Main Street.

Still another successful rose in Mangham is one I collected from the
Chelsea Physic Garden in London in the early 2000s. It has thrived and
blooms almost continuously with large, China-like crimson flowers. In a
recent article in *Gardens Illustrated* magazine (issue 228), it is referred to
as "a remarkable, relatively thornless China rose that flowers at the Chelsea
Physic Garden almost all year round." Its image is captioned "*Rosa × odorata*
(Sanguinea Group) 'Bengal Crimson.'"

A number of island beds in the garden look especially nice in late winter

Phlox pilosa, or
prairie phlox, has
been tucked into
the flower beds
here and there to
provide continuity.

Jesse Lee Harris has maintained the Mangham gardens for many years.

and spring when the bulbs rotate through the seasons. One of the nicest and most enduring combinations was planted by Jessie Lee around several of the big old pecan trees in the backyard. The circles begin with 'Grand Primo' and *Narcissus × italicus*, snowflakes (*Leucojum aestivum*), and old-fashioned daylilies (*Hemerocallis fulva*). In late summer, hundreds of red spider lilies (*Lycoris radiata*) suddenly appear after early fall rain showers.

The west boundary of the property is screened with sasanqua camellias obtained from the late Aubrey King of King's Nursery in Tenaha, Texas. We aren't sure of the cultivar name, but they are grown from cuttings from his family plantings. They are semidouble pink with yellow stamens and are now about eight feet tall and wide. Anchoring each end of this hedge are large specimens of Chinese fringe trees, also from King's Nursery. Aubrey also provided me with several choice camellias including 'Governor Mouton.'

Dr. Dave Creech at Stephen F. Austin State University in Nacogdoches, Texas, has shared many plants over the years. Recently, I transplanted two specimens of *Chionanthus retusus* 'Tokyo Tower,' which is a fastigiate (upright) type of Chinese fringe tree. I grew these for several years at Twin Oaks and they never flowered. Dr. Creech speculates that this selection needs more chilling hours and will probably flower in Mangham, so we dug them up and moved them.

Under a grove of dogwood in the front yard is a specimen of Ruth Knopf's "Peach Tea." It is cream colored with a bit of peachy blush. These contrast beautifully with the rosy, bright-eyed masses of *Phlox paniculata* 'John Fanick.' These begin flowering in midsummer and continue through the fall. Another mass of dogwood in the front garden includes a twelve-

The soft shades
of the Byzantine
gladiolus and
the prairie phlox
blend nicely
with the pastel
colors of antique
bricks in this
Mangham back
garden area.

to fifteen-foot-tall specimen of *Magnolia macrophylla* (bigleaf magnolia) given to us by Greg's friends Jerrell and Darrell Durham, who are twins and amateur nurserymen in Lufkin, Texas. Another flowering tree of interest is a *Sinojackia* hybrid from Cynthia Mueller that blooms with *Styrax*-like white flowers in spring.

Camellias really thrive in the Mangham garden. There are a couple dozen old plants that were probably planted in the 1920s or 1930s. Even during extreme dry spells when azaleas and other hardy shrubs suffer, camellias seem to take it in their stride. Our neighbor, the late Bobby McDonald, loved camellias and was a member of the Camellia Society in Monroe. He enjoyed growing and grafting them in our garden. Bobby also planted a hedge of *Viburnum macrophyllum* (bigleaf viburnum) along the east side of our property. They have matured into a fifteen- to twenty-foot hedge that helps create privacy in the middle of town.

Camellias first arrived in America in about 1800 and were grown as hothouse plants in Philadelphia. Their true potential emerged when adventuresome gardeners planted them outside in Savannah and Charleston. Our Mangham garden is defined largely by camellias, azaleas, spring-flowering bulbs, roses, and dogwoods. There were no dogwoods on the property when we acquired it. The originals came from Emory Smith's Hilltop Nursery in Baton Rouge. Mr. Smith was famous for his knowledge and collections of native Louisiana plants. He shared what he considered a superior strain of flowering dogwood (*Cornus florida*), which thrived and reseeded prolifically on our property. Jessie Lee continually repots seedlings, which we share with other gardening friends.

Pebble Creek

Like many homeowners today, we decided to build on a smaller property in College Station to reduce maintenance, but also to take advantage of a golf course view. Although only about 80 feet wide and 120 feet deep, our rear views from the house are unobstructed. We have a zero lot line on one side and adjoin a green space on the other, which helps give us some breathing room since there will never be construction there.

Another objective was to have considerable outdoor living and entertaining space. This resulted in no lawn except on the street side, where landscape design is coordinated by the housing development and lawn and garden maintenance is provided by the home owners' association.

The Welch Pebble Creek "zero-lot-line" home.

A gazebo is the architectural focus of the side garden. It is designed to feature climbing roses and is about twenty feet tall at its highest point. I chose the yellow Lady Banks and set out two plants on opposite corners of the twelve-foot-square structure. They have grown quickly and make an impressive exhibit each spring. They also provide cooling shade during the warm months. After fifteen years of growing there they became overgrown, so I pruned them severely last year. This seemed a bit excessive at the time, but within a few months the plants began recovering and the extra light was really appreciated by the satsumas and kumquats planted nearby. We have had a huge crop of satsumas and kumquats this winter and the rose looks fine. The house provides protection from north winds and allows us to grow the citrus and other tropical plants with little or no protection.

Only fifteen feet separate our house from the solid brick wall of our neighbor. This has provided an opportunity to design and build ornamental iron trellises that provide continuing color in a relatively small space. The trellises extend about seventy-five feet and are six feet tall. Since they are in raised beds they are actually a bit taller. The first forty feet of the trellises are completely covered with Greg's recently found climbing sport of 'Belinda's Dream.' These bloom profusely during spring with perfectly formed, large, fully-petaled dark pink flowers. Their fragrance is as pleasant as that of their parent, 'Belinda's Dream.'

Lady Banks roses are very vigorous growers. This climber is held in place by an iron gazebo structure, providing filtered shade for the many containers and somewhat tender plants growing underneath.

These trellises serve as a wall in the motor court area that is adjacent to our garage and also serve as an entry walk to our front courtyard. For many years I have enjoyed several large clay pots with 'Marie Pavié' roses in them. A cluster of several large clay pots with seasonal color serve as accents in the motor court area. I first encountered 'Marie Pavié' on my initial visit to the rose garden at the Huntington Botanical Gardens. I brought a small plant on the plane trip back from that visit and provided it for stock at the Antique Rose Emporium. Its small size, continuous bloom, and intense fragrance make it one of my (and Greg's) all-time favorites.

Renovations were made in the Pebble Creek garden a little more than a year ago. These included adding a specimen of "Katy Road Pink" and an island bed with several plants of 'Belinda's Dream' and a single plant of "Peggy Martin," surrounded by a mass of 'Mrs. James Hendry' crinums and drifts of red and yellow lycoris from Chris Wiesinger (Southern Bulb Company). The "Peggy Martin" rose is being trained up the trunk of a medium-sized post oak. Although known for their mass of flowers in spring, my "Peggy Martin" roses have bloomed well this past fall.

The front courtyard is separated from the motor court by a four-foot-tall brick wall and an iron gate. The iron trellises continue into this space, where a pool and fountain provide the sound of moving water, and pots of water cannas and Louisiana iris add color and a defined entrance. A large specimen of 'Prosperity' rose provides huge masses of white flowers in spring and continuous flowering throughout the growing season.

Another rose arbor just beyond the gazebo is covered with 'Reve d'Or.' There is something special about the peachy-rose coloring of that rose that I

'Prosperity' rose is a mannerly climber well suited to trellises.

A view from the porch area, looking out onto the golf course. Byzantine gladiolus, old-fashioned petunias, and "Peggy Martin" roses contribute their color to the plantings.

find captivating. An antique iron urn sits beneath the 'Reve d'Or' arch. Potted plant arrangements feature numerous succulents and topiaries. I have trained variegated English ivy that I grew from cuttings from Frances Parker on a wire pyramid. Frances and her husband, Milton, are longtime friends. She is a great gardener and has shared many roses and other plants from her beautiful garden in Beaufort, South Carolina.

For about fifteen years, we enjoyed eight-foot-tall iron obelisks mounted on brick bases that were covered with "Peggy Martin" roses. Last year I moved the obelisks to the ends of the garden and planted coral vine (*Antigonon leptopus*), a favorite perennial vine, on them. In addition to the four obelisks, the garden now relies on 'Scarlet's Peak,' a female fastigiate (upright) yaupon holly, for vertical interest. I have become intrigued with this plant because of its dark red berries and strong vertical form. I have a pair of them at the stair going down to the golf course level of the rear garden and another pair near the front gate. In gardens like ours at Pebble Creek where space is limited, trellises, gazebos, and arched structures provide visual impact usually found only in larger gardens.

Small-flowered narcissus, Byzantine gladiolus, and perennial chrysanthemums share the flower bed and provide seasonal color in rotation (image courtesy of Ralph Anderson).

The raised area contains a sixty-foot-long bed filled with Greg's 'Marie Daly' roses. They are spaced about four feet apart and grow to about three to four feet tall. They provide some organization to the planting that includes random placement of Byzantine gladiolus from both Greg and Chris Wiesinger. Clumps of garden mums provide fall color. These include 'Country Girl' (single, pale pink) and an extremely vigorous, beautiful, anemone-flowered white mum from Greg that he named "Mildred Golden" after the woman who once lived on the old homesite where he found it. Mildred was Greg's paternal grandmother's sister's first husband's mother!

The lower level of the garden has four very large cement pots filled with spineless prickly pear, Greg's *Setcreasea* 'Pale Puma,' and *Calylophus berlandieri* with its masses of bright yellow flowers spring through fall. Between each of the four large pots are four plants of 'Belinda's Dream' roses. These provide not only almost continuous color in the garden, but also armloads of cut flowers for display inside the house.

Seasonal color is set out twice each year in the front garden as a service of the home owners' association. Pansies are the cool-season choice and periwinkles in various colors during the summer. I supplement these with pink, purple, and lavender snapdragons, 'Laura Bush' petunias, wax-leaf begonias, and chartreuse-green sweet potato. Masses of 'Mrs. James Hendry' crinum are planted at the bases of the 'Scarlet's Peak' yaupon, while *Narcissus* × *italicus*, *N.* 'Grand Primo,' and *N.* × 'Golden Dawn' add early spring interest and brighten the front garden.

Twin Oaks

After Diane passed away, I married Lucille Presley. Lucille spent most of her career in Houston but is a Washington County native. She and her late husband built a retirement home near Independence, not far from where she grew up and just down the road from the homes of her parents and grandparents. Her place is only a few miles from the Antique Rose Emporium, where she enjoyed visiting and purchasing plants as she landscaped her home. She has always had a large vegetable garden that produces well in her sandy soil. Although I loved Fragilee, also in Washington County, it didn't seem feasible to have two homes in the area. I was heartened when the first couple who looked at Fragilee bought it instantly and gave me permission to visit, photograph, and take cuttings at any time.

Lucille named her place "Twin Oaks" for the two giant live oaks near the house, which is on a high spot providing views for miles around. On a clear

Twin Oaks, the
Washington
County, Texas,
country home
of the Welches
(image courtesy of
Ralph Anderson).

day we can see Kyle Field at Texas A&M University, which is about forty miles away. She is a dedicated and talented gardener. At her Houston home, she had beautiful azaleas and was committed to having them at Twin Oaks as well. By hauling truckloads of pine needles to mulch and help acidify the soil, she has healthy 'Formosa' azaleas across the entire front of her house. They do require irrigation during our long, hot summers but generally perform well. Lucille also has a nice rose garden that features some of the same roses I enjoy such as 'Old Blush,' "Caldwell Pink," 'Ducher,' 'Carefree Beauty,' 'Mrs. Dudley Cross,' and 'Belinda's Dream,' which is her favorite in the garden and as cut flowers. She is active in the Bluebonnet Garden Club of Brenham, which hosts events in the community and operates within the Texas Garden Clubs organization.

I had never had a place to successfully grow vegetables and was pleased to have my own space, as well as an area where we both gardened. We grow tomatoes, potatoes, eggplant, okra, peppers, lettuce, green beans, and more. There was no attempt to organize the vegetable garden, and some fruit trees were also included. Lucille had always had a few peach trees, an ancient and remarkable pear, and a very old 'Green Ischia' fig. Tim Hartmann, Extension Program specialist and good friend, has helped and encouraged us by

Large, venerable old live oaks are one of the most attractive features of the country landscape in this area of Texas (image courtesy of Ralph Anderson).

budding pears, grapefruit, peaches, and Japanese persimmons. He has also shared fig cuttings and helped in pruning the fruit trees.

There is a nice large metal barn that provides storage for tractors, farm equipment, lawn mowers, and various equipment to support the hay business on the land. Another small metal building known as "The Shed" contained garden-related tools, fertilizers, and so forth. This building was deteriorating, with parts of the roof becoming loose and foundation timbers showing signs of decay. We decided that a new "shed" was needed. We consulted Bob Ruth, ASLA, a longtime friend and landscape architect. Since Lucille originally sought Bob's advice in the early stages of landscaping on the property and he was a longtime colleague of mine, we thought it would be fitting to have him involved in enlarging the outdoor living area at the back of the house, remodeling the "summer house" (a fifteen-by-twenty-foot screened structure for outdoor dining, etc.), and designing a new shed.

Lucille is also a good chef and enjoys canning, freezing, and experimenting with fresh fruit and produce from the garden. We decided to enlarge the concept of the existing shed and include a kitchen, food storage area, and guest facilities. We also chose to create a garden that would feature the vegetables, herbs, roses, and a growing collection of fruit trees.

Soon after Lucille and I married, we took a trip to England to attend

The front of the "new shed" intended for housing overnight guests and entertaining.

the Chelsea Flower Show and visit the Isle of Jersey to tour gardens. This was my second visit to Jersey, as I had gone previously with Chris Wiesinger and his family regarding collaboration with a pottery maker. There are many beautiful gardens on Jersey, and two of them have influenced my ideas about garden design. One of these was at the home of Susan Lee. The garden was beautifully designed and overlooked the ocean with a view of the coast of France. Probably the most stunning part was a 150-foot-long border of flowering shrubs and perennials. Also fascinating was a walled garden just out from the house that included a remarkable feature inspired by the French. Sue called this garden her "Spanish garden." A beautiful water feature and many attractive shrubs and flowering trees greeted visitors. The main focus of the garden was a beautifully constructed entrance from the center of the space to what looked like a grand entrance to another "room" in her garden. As we neared this elaborate entrance, we suddenly realized it wasn't an entrance at all, but a mirror that created the illusion of going through space. The French have a word for this: trompe l'oeil. The literal translation is "fool the eye." It certainly fooled mine!

I had taken a number of photos of Susan Lee's garden and shared one of the images of the trompe l'oeil with Bob Ruth. We had been trying to come up with an idea to add some formality to our new vegetable garden, and Bob said he knew a craftsperson who could do that for us. Of course, there were some differences. Independence, Texas, is not the Isle of Jersey, and our metal barn wasn't an obvious choice for the termination of a formal axis in our garden, but we decided to give it a try. The woodwork creating the false illusion in front of the mirror was well done. It was the center of a grape arbor covered in "Peggy Martin" and "Queenie" roses in the center and 'Champanel' grapes extending another fifteen feet or so on both sides. Stepping-stones of native limestone were set in front of the mirror and succulents were planted among them.

  The walk toward the trompe l'oeil is intersected by a six-foot-diameter circle of plantings centered on an old piece of garden sculpture filled with rain lilies and seasonal bulbs and encircled by a clipped hedge of boxwood. To the right is a stone bench and arbor covered with 'Zephirine Drouhin' roses. Their thornless stems and brilliant cerise/pink flowers are spectacu-

The newly envisioned trompe l'oeil, flanked by annual larkspur and dill. "Peggy Martin" roses are just beginning their full flush of flowering in the background (image courtesy of Ralph Anderson).

ABOVE: The
stone wall with
'Old Blush" roses
(image courtesy of
Ralph Anderson).

ABOVE RIGHT:
Iris × albicans
(cemetery white
iris).

lar in spring and there are occasional flowers in summer and fall. The exact
same arch and rose planting lies between the round bed on the axis line
and the trompe l'oeil. The arches of the structures again repeat those in the
new "shed." At appropriate points along the axis line to the trompe l'oeil are
clipped topiaries of dwarf myrtle (*Myrtus communis* 'Compacta'). These were
obtained from a gardening friend in Schulenburg and are finally reaching a
noticeable size. All this area is planted in seasonal vegetables and reseeding
petunias, cockscombs, larkspurs, and poppies.

One of Bob Ruth's many contributions to the landscape was a series of
stone walls similar to those constructed by German immigrants to Texas 150
or more years ago. These walls span a total of about five hundred linear feet
and are about two feet tall and eighteen inches wide. They are ornamental
but also help facilitate drainage and provide seating. They appear as "dry
stack" native stone walls but actually contain some mortar. One of these is
offset from the "shed" about one hundred feet to the north and includes a
row of 'Old Blush' roses. It is bordered by cemetery white iris (*Iris × albi-*

cans) that were handed down to Lucille from her grandfather. 'Golden Dawn' narcissus is also planted as part of the edging for the roses. The combination is stunning when the roses and iris are in bloom. Sometimes they bloom simultaneously and sometimes not, but either way they are a huge source of low-maintenance color.

The plantings in front of the "shed" are flanked by two raised stone planters with matching specimens of 'Scarlet's Peak' yaupon holly. A ten-foot row of "Katy Road Pink" roses encloses a somewhat formal space that includes a seven-foot-diameter metal cattle watering trough lined with clipped boxwood and centered on a copper fountain. Seasonal color featuring larkspurs, snapdragons, summer phlox, and low-maintenance containers of succulents completes the front garden.

The arch of this gate is framed with 'Zepherine Drouhin' roses. Blackberries in bloom cover the fence, and old-fashioned petunias add annual color to the foreground (image courtesy of Ralph Anderson).

'Old Blush' roses, Iris × albicans (cemetery white iris), and Narcissus × italicus grow well together and provide several seasons of color (image courtesy of Ralph Anderson).

Twin Oaks has been a fun project that we especially enjoy sharing with friends in the spring when the entire locale becomes a wildflower destination and our roses are in full bloom. Our front gate is covered with "Peggy Martin" roses bordered with *Narcissus × italicus*. Traffic on Highway 390 is heavy with city dwellers from Houston and other communities enjoying the countryside and wildflowers. Our "Peggy Martin" roses at the front gate have been known to slow down or completely stop traffic.

All of the gardens that I developed have brought joy and granted unique insight into rose cultivation. Generally, I encourage companion planting with roses for a complete effect. Natural companions for old roses are heirloom bulbs such as 'Grand Primo' narcissus, St. Joseph's lily, crinums, snowflakes, and rain lilies. I often plant clumps or masses of rosemary, ornamental sages (salvias) in shades of blue, pink, white, and purple, and silvery plants such as *Artemisia* 'Powis Castle,' lavender, agaves, and sedums to complement roses. Rose mallows (*Hibiscus* × 'Lady Baltimore' and 'Peppermint Flare') can be coordinated with roses of similar or contrasting colors. Masses of low-growing roses like "Martha Gonzales" and "Caldwell Pink" are excellent choices as transition plants to larger-growing shrub types. Certain combinations, whether they enhance or contrast with roses, will give the garden more definition and interest.

WRAP-UP

Greg Grant

Antique roses aren't good because they're old, they're old because they're good.
— GREG GRANT

My dear friend and mentor Dr. Jerry Parsons of San Antonio always said there are two kinds of people in this world—those who grow roses, and those who wish they grew roses. After all, roses are arguably the most popular flower in the world and are technically our national flower. Unfortunately, however, for more than half my lifetime, the majority of roses available to gardeners would grow only if you made them grow. Now who would think that scenario would invite another generation to grow roses? Hooray for level-

Most rose gardens are full of roses that don't want to grow.

headed gardeners like William Robertson, Gertrude Jekyll, Pam Puryear, and Ruth Knopf, who were able to buck current popularity and periodically announce, "The Emperor is naked; we left all the good flowers behind."

Roses didn't start out as wimpy flowers. Humans did that to them. In addition to being beautiful in a simplistic way, roses were initially wiry and mean as snakes. This made them perfect Texans, of course. If an antique rose is still around, it's because it's tough and because it's pretty. Those are the two most important attributes of a rose. And make no mistake about it—toughness is more important than beauty. If you don't believe me, then hold a beauty contest between a white five-petaled wild rose and a dead rose that was supposed to have a hundred red petals swirled into a gargantuan blossom! I'm not making this up. I've lived it.

If you don't think that roses are inherently tough as nails, just look at invasive roses like the Macartney rose or multiflora rose spreading across the country. Or admire wild roses like the prairie rose and swamp rose, which have been growing on their own in America for thousands of years. This genetic toughness still resides within the best of the antique roses—those that have survived to tell their stories, those that our ancestors brought with them as they headed west across America and that our grandmothers and their grandmothers tended with pans of dishwater near the front porches of simple

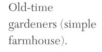

Old-time gardeners (simple farmhouse).

If Southerners love roses they take them in as their own and share them as long as they live. This late-winter bouquet features "Satin Cream Tea," 'Ducher,' and an assortment of fragrant early narcissus.

farmhouses. These folks had much more to worry about than trying to keep roses alive. Yet roses they had.

To me, the secrets these roses keep are just as important as the roses themselves. Once a lady at one of my lectures said, "My plants don't have stories like yours do." I stopped her right there and let her know that all plants have stories. Just because you don't know them doesn't mean that they don't exist. As a card-carrying Texan with a birthright for "truth distortion," I told her if she couldn't dig up any stories on them, I'd be happy to make some up for her!

Heirloom pass-along roses have proven their worth time and again. The fact that they are still around proves that they are adaptive and want to grow. Gardening in the South is tough; if roses aren't able to survive floods, tornadoes, hurricanes, blue northers, heat waves, blistering drought, livestock, and inebriated relatives, then we don't want them. If they grow for us and we like the way they look, we adopt them, take them in as our own, and share them as long as we live—and beyond. They've more than earned the right to be saved, cherished, and have their stories told.

ACKNOWLEDGMENTS

There are many people to thank for my life in gardening and roses, and for this book. For those that I've inadvertently left out, I promise to plant a rose on their grave. If that won't do, they can stand in line and dance on mine. First, I'd like to thank my coauthor and mentor, Dr. William C. Welch. Without him, my life wouldn't have been the same, culturally or horticulturally. He made me not only a gardener, but a writer as well. A huge debt of eternal thanks also goes to my other living mentor, Dr. Jerry Parsons. He enthusiastically taught me both basic and advanced horticulture but, even more importantly, plant propagation and commercial horticulture. And with the brains of Einstein, the humor of Jerry Clower, and the mouth of a sailor, he lured me into the exciting world of new plant development and introduction. Dr. Welch and Dr. Parsons both introduced me to Texas AgriLife Extension. I was born a county agent.

A special thank-you to my parents, Neil and Jackie Grant, for letting me play in the dirt and calling me back in when the sun went down each day. A million loving thanks to my Granny Ruth and Grandmother Emanis for teaching me to love flowers, people, and my roots. Eternal gratitude goes to my late first-grade teacher, Mozelle Johnston, for sharing her love of life, plants, and painting with me. Loving thanks to the late Marie and Autry Daly for letting me mow their huge lawn in Longview when I was a boy. I would have done it for free. I will go to my grave missing them. A million thank-yous to my late friend Pamela Ashworth Puryear, who taught me it was okay to march backward to the beat of your own drum. She offered me a lifetime of encouragement. Thank you to Shreveport's late Cleo Barnwell for sharing her roses, bulbs, wildflowers, books, and friends with me. Thank you as well to the late Eddie and John Fanick for sharing their wisdom, family, friendship, plants, and legendary San Antonio nursery with me. A large debt of thanks also goes to the late Aubrey King and his one-hundred-year-old King's Nursery in Tenaha for sharing his friendship, family, and plants with me. As far as I'm concerned, Aubrey is still here. A multitude of thanks are owed to the late Flora Ann Bynum and her Southern Garden History Society. She was the nicest, smartest, most gracious person I ever knew.

Many more thanks go to Felder Rushing for sharing his philosophy, friendship, and Greenwood Cemetery with me. I also want to thank my Cousin Celia for sharing her love of flowers and life with me. A heartfelt thank-you goes to my friend Missy for encouraging me to love roses again. A heaping thanks to rose rustler Becky Smith for sharing her roses and iris with me and also for encouraging the writing of this book and the preservation of Pam Puryear's memory. A big thank-you to Mike Shoup and his Antique Rose Emporium for providing me with my very first inspirational job while I was at Texas A&M and for letting us use a number of his beautiful images for this book. Thanks to Bill Jobe for allowing me to use his garden for my constant flow of experimental plants, and to his lovely wife, Mary Louise, for feeding me a delicious lunch every week. If I look like a butterball it's because of Mary Louise and my Momma. Thank you to Jason Powell and his Petals from the Past Nursery for sharing his family, plants, and nursery with me. Jason and I both tutored under Dr. Welch and are kindred spirits. A big thank-you to Mitzi VanSant for sharing her early memories of the Texas Rose Rustlers with Bill and me. Much appreciation goes to Neil Sperry for letting me write for him for thirty years and to *Texas Gardener* Magazine for allowing me to tell my stories in each issue. Many thanks go to Beverly Welch and the Arbor Gate Nursery for letting me wax philosophical in a monthly blog.

An immense debt of gratitude is owed to friend and Texas A&M computer geek Paul Greer for saving my unfinished manuscript from a deceased computer. Without Paul, you'd be reading this book telepathically from blank pages. Also a big rat terrier kiss to friend Cynthia Mueller for coordinating Dr. Welch and me two hundred miles apart. Continued thanks go to longtime friend Cara Day for editing not only this book but also all my monthly scribblings. Cara Day and Becky Smith won't leave me be until I've shared my tell-all letters from Pam Puryear in a beauty-shop book one day, so be prepared. And finally, thank you to Texas A&M University Press and Shannon Davies for once again giving me the opportunity to share my tall tales with the world. As a proud Texas Aggie, I couldn't be happier.

—GREG GRANT

Gardening is contagious! Many longtime friendships begin in the garden. Gardeners have an immediate affinity for each other's interests, as well as their plant treasures. Sharing plants and knowledge is a natural inclination that helps build a sense of appreciation and a feeling that transcends barriers of wealth, class, and social connections. I have always made a practice of sharing starts of plants or information on how they may be grown in order to "plant a seed of gardening interest." My gardening interest began very early and is described in this book as it relates to roses in particular. Several mentors have helped focus my interest.

One of these mentors was Lynn Lowrey, whom I first met as a teenager in Houston. While well known for his work with native plants, Lynn also experimented with many Asian plants like crapemyrtles, Callery pears, Chinese fringe trees, and tough roses like Lady Banks and *Rosa × fortuniana*. While working with Lynn, I learned to appreciate mayhaws, pawpaws, huckleberries, persimmons, native crabapples, berries, and other members of the rose family.

Another Houston influence important to me was Paul Robinson, owner of Paul's Green Thumb Nursery, which was prominent at the time. I worked there as a young teenager on weekends. Paul was a great marketer and sold huge quantities of Tyler roses, which he received bare root in January, immediately planted in containers, and sold during late winter and early spring. These were basically hybrid teas but included a few old favorites like 'Paul's Scarlet,' 'Paul Neyron,' 'American Beauty,' and 'Red and Pink Radiance.'

Another important mentor was Dr. Robert Reich, head of the Landscape Architecture Department at Louisiana State University (LSU). Dr. Reich had a monumental effect on landscape architecture across the nation. He taught many important life lessons and was able to bring out the best in even those students thought to be the least promising. This made a great impression on me, and I have always tried to follow his example of helping people to find their own potential. His guidance and support in my career and those of hundreds of others has made a huge mark.

Among others I met during college and learned greatly from was Emory Smith, who had a small nursery on Highland Road in Baton Rouge. Emory Smith and his family left their beautiful property to the Landscape Architecture Department at LSU and it has become Hilltop Arboretum, which makes outstanding contributions to the people of Baton Rouge and the Landscape Architecture Program at LSU.

Outstanding students I have encountered and encouraged at Texas A&M

have been a joy in my career. Jason Powell and his future wife, Shelley, were both graduate students here in the 1990s. After completing his undergraduate degree at Auburn, Jason came here to work on a master's degree in pomology. That was when I was developing the landscape at Cricket Court, our former country home in Washington County. Jason was very helpful in the development and maintenance of the gardens there and became very interested in the nearby Antique Rose Emporium, which he visited regularly. After he and Shelley married, they moved back to Alabama and started Petals from the Past Nursery near Jemison. The gardens at Petals from the Past are nationally known for their connections with gardening, their suitability as a wedding destination, and the opportunity they provide to experience roses, fresh fruit, and a beautiful site.

Mike Shoup was working on a master's degree here in the Horticulture Department when we first met. He had a nursery focused on native plants in Independence, Texas. Through the resulting Antique Rose Emporium, the public was able to obtain the interesting and hard-to-get early garden roses that are now so popular. The retail garden center became an important destination for events and tours.

Greg Grant is my nomination for the "most unique creation" of the Horticulture Department here at Texas A&M. Greg continues to evolve and amaze his many friends. From our first meeting in my office when he came to me as an undergraduate with a stem of his great-grandmother's tea rose to identify, our friendship has been a lasting and dynamic one. Somehow I feel that in years to come Greg will continue to produce joy and excitement for all of us.

Chris Wiesinger and I also met in my office as he began to pursue his interests in heirloom bulbs as a student project in Dr. Fred Davies's class. His plan to specialize in bulbs for the South has succeeded wonderfully, and he continues to discover fresh troves of historical bulbs and make them available to the gardening public. We worked hard together to produce *The Bulb Hunter* and still enjoy appearing together for lectures and demonstrations on how to grow and combine bulbs, well-chosen perennials, and old garden roses.

Tim Hartmann was lured over from "the dark side" (fruit tree breeding) to landscape horticulture after my attempts at brainwashing. Tim is currently a program specialist in Earth-Kind® here in Extension Horticulture. He has never met a stranger and is an inspirational teacher of plant propagation and edible plants. I expect that Tim has a very bright future as an extension educator. He is a source of inspiration to his coworkers and students.

Pam Puryear was an inspirational friend and historian who helped develop the structure of our interest in old garden roses, their names, and origins. She was dogged with her research and helped me with historical data and primary source information for my early books and articles on roses, cottage gardens, and early Texas nurseries.

Our mutual friend Aubrey King, his wife, Cheryl, and oldest son, Andrew, gave generously of their time and plant material for the many horticultural occasions we presented. King's Nursery in Tenaha, Texas, has been in business for one hundred years, and its East Texas location has allowed it to specialize in regionally adapted plants. Large specimens of old roses such as 'Climbing Cecile Brunner' and 'Reve d'Or' continue to welcome customers who are drawn to the nursery because of its innovative offerings and the generous nature of the King family.

Organizations have continued to provide welcome support through mutual interests and lasting friendships. The Garden Club of America, the National Garden Club and its Texas affiliate Texas Garden Clubs, Inc., and the Master Gardener chapters throughout the South have provided a wonderful support system for sharing garden knowledge and contacts. The Southern Garden History Society and its two late founding figures, William Lanier Hunt and Flora Ann Bynum, continue to inspire and propel us forward in the quest for knowledge of our gardening heritage. Staci Catron, director of the Cherokee Garden Library of Atlanta, Georgia, is a dynamic leader in the Southern Garden History Society and an authority on the written history of Southern gardening.

Cynthia Wickizer Mueller has provided valuable editorial assistance, historical anecdotes, and "factoids" for sixteen years. She continues to volunteer in my office and provides useful and fun revelations. Cynthia has propagated many of the "rose finds" such as Elizabeth Lawrence's white Lady Banks and "Peggy Martin." She has also shared many crinums, bulbs, myrtles, boxwoods, and perennials.

My wife, Lucille, is a serious gardener herself and brings lifelong gardening experience. She turns our vegetable and fruit crops into remarkable pickles, jellies, and jams and plans wonderful dinner parties and garden events. Our garden at Twin Oaks has been a joy, as has our relationship with Bob Ruth, ASLA, as we planned and implemented our new garden. My son Will, his wife, Mandy, and their "perfect" daughters, Kathlyn Alyse and Ella Diane, bring joy to our lives and love to pose for pictures. My late wife, Diane, although not a serious gardener, loved our gardening friends and was a great facilitator. She lives on in our granddaughters.

The Texas AgriLife Extension Service has provided unstinting opportunity and support throughout the years. The genius of the land-grant university system continues to prove its worth in our changing times. Dr. Douglas Steele, director of the Texas AgriLife Extension Service, is committed to taking the latest from our land-grant university to every community in Texas and makes each of us feel that we are an important part of that process. Our network of county horticulturists and specialists, including Dr. Dan Lineburger, head of our Horticulture Department, and Dr. Larry Stein, project supervisor for Extension Horticulture, provide leadership, interest, and support to our projects.

Many thanks go to Shannon Davies, director, and the staff of Texas A&M University Press for their encouragement, insights, and help loading my heavy book boxes!

—BILL WELCH

EARTH-KIND® ROSES

Earth-Kind® is a special designation given to select rose cultivars by the Texas A&M AgriLife Extension Service through the Earth-Kind® landscaping program. It is based on the results of extensive research and field trials and is awarded only to those roses demonstrating superior pest tolerance, combined with outstanding landscape performance. The following information is from the website http://aggie-horticulture.tamu.edu/earthkindroses/cultivars/.

Dwarf Shrubs

'Marie Daly'—'Marie Daly' is a pink sport of the renowned old garden rose 'Marie Pavié.' It was first identified in Arcadia, Texas, by Greg Grant. This delightful polyantha is covered with very fragrant, semidouble pink flowers that can turn almost white during periods of intense heat. It blooms spring through fall and is well mannered, with a graceful rounded form. 'Marie Daly' has few thorns and is wonderful for high-traffic areas and places where children may play. 'Marie Daly' can be very useful in the landscape as a mass planting, low hedge, or specimen plant. It also does very well in a container where it benefits from excellent air circulation. It is resistant to spider mite problems.

'Marie Daly.'

'Souvenir de St. Anne's'—This sport of 'Souvenir de la Malmaison' was bred in England by Thomas Hilling. It was found in St. Anne's Park, Dublin. The pale pink petals glow with translucent beauty and are very fragrant. It is an excellent choice for mass plantings and borders. Few hips are produced. This cultivar is so outstanding that it was named "Earth-Kind® Rose of the Year" for 2009 by the Texas AgriLife Extension Service.

'Souvenir de St. Anne's' (image courtesy of Mike Shoup).

'The Fairy.'

'The Fairy'—'The Fairy' was first introduced in 1932 and has been popular ever since because of its small size, abundant pink blooms, and tough nature. It produces a wealth of small, double, light pink blossoms that may turn blush white during intense heat. Its foliage is bright green, shiny, and very attractive. 'The Fairy' is very useful for small landscapes because of its size, with a mature height of three feet and a width of four feet. It has a low, spreading habit that is great for softening harsh angles or cascading over the edge of a container. It is outstanding in a massed planting to fill a central bed that is surrounded by a walkway in an Earth-Kind® rose garden or as a border spilling over the front edge of a landscape bed.

Small Shrubs

"Caldwell Pink."

"Caldwell Pink"—The proper identification of this rose is a mystery. Some rosarians speculate that it could be 'Pink Pet.' Sometimes it is referred to as the "Summer Carnation Rose." Disease and heat tolerance are high in this rose. It prefers well-drained amended soils but will tolerate alkaline clay soils. It is a graceful plant with a leafy spreading habit that produces shoots bearing clusters of twenty to fifty flowers one and a half inches wide. "Caldwell Pink" is very useful in the landscape as a border, hedge, or specimen plant.

'Cecile Brunner'—'Cecile Brunner,' also known as 'Mlle. Cecile Brunner' and the sweetheart rose, is a bush rose that grows to four feet. It blooms profusely in the spring and continues to bloom until frost. Blossoms are a soft silvery pink and look like those of a hybrid tea in miniature. They appear in clusters and have a sweet fragrance. The plant is upright and bushy with dark green, slightly shiny leaves. Foliage is soft with sparse thorns. It requires little pruning. This is one of the best loved and easiest to grow of roses.

'Cecile Brunner,' sweetheart rose.

'Perle d'Or'—'Perle d'Or' (pearl of gold) is a highly regarded old garden rose that is well suited to many growing conditions, even alkaline clay soil and hot, dry weather. It blooms from spring until fall and replaces spent flowers quickly with new flushes of bloom. It does not like to be too wet, nor does it appreciate highly saline irrigation water. This rose works well anywhere in the landscape that has good air circulation. It is also suitable for a large container on a deck or patio or along a walkway where its fragrance and flowers can be enjoyed up close. 'Perle d'Or' was selected as the 2007 "Earth-Kind® Rose of the Year" by the Texas AgriLife Extension Service.

Medium Shrubs

'Perle d'Or.'

    'Belinda's Dream'—Introduced in 1992, this gorgeous shrub rose was developed by the late Dr. Robert Basye, a retired mathematics professor at Texas A&M University, and named after the daughter of one of his friends. 'Belinda's Dream' is disease tolerant and has gorgeous flowers. Used as a specimen plant, a hedge, or even in a large pot, this rose has the impact and beauty of a hybrid tea but is much more disease and soil tolerant. It was the first rose to be designated Earth-Kind® by the Texas AgriLife Extension Service. The large, very double pink blossoms come in large clusters from spring until frost. Bred in Texas to withstand hot temperatures, it does well in temperate climates as well. It may have some black spot in cool, damp weather, but its vigor and blooming will not be affected by the disease. Light pruning improves appearance and blooming frequency.

'Belinda's Dream' (image courtesy of Ralph Anderson).

    'Carefree Beauty'—One of the best of the shrub roses developed by Dr. Griffith Buck at Iowa State University to withstand the long, cold winters of the Midwest, 'Carefree Beauty' has also proven to be an excellent choice for gardens in Texas that are challenged by hot, dry summers. 'Carefree Beauty' was named 2006 "Earth-Kind® Rose of the Year" by the Texas AgriLife Extension Service and is also recommended by the University of Minnesota. Introduced in 1977, this rose was known in Texas for a number of years as "Katy Road Pink" after it was found on Katy Road in Houston by early Texas Rose Rustlers. It produces successive flushes of deep rich pink blos-

"Katy Road Pink."

soms fast and furiously from spring until frost. The flowers open flat with a few irregular, loose petals at the center and an occasional white stripe running through them. Large orange hips are produced from nearly every flower.

'Ducher.'

'Duchesse de Brabant.'

'Else Poulsen' (image courtesy of Mike Shoup).

"Georgetown Tea."

The rich color of the shrub makes it a natural choice for use in groupings of three to five plants wherever you want the viewer's eye to be drawn.

'Ducher'—Bred in Lyon, France, by Jean-Claude Ducher in 1869, 'Ducher' (pronounced "doo-shay") is one of a very few white China roses. While the Ducher family bred many lovely roses over a lengthy period, this modest rose is the one they chose to bear their family name. Petals of the medium-sized blooms are pure white, though the light reflected often takes on a creamy color. The bush has been described as looking like snow in a pine forest. The double blooms have a fruity fragrance. The compact, rounded, twiggy bush is a nice landscape shrub either as a specimen plant or in a drift of three to five plants. The soft fullness of the foliage and showy flowers make this an excellent choice to blend with more structured shrubs in a landscape. As one of the smaller China roses, it also works well in a large pot. 'Ducher' tolerates heat, sun, and various soil conditions.

'Duchesse de Brabant'—Long-lasting fragrance and full-cupped, repetitious bloom set 'Duchesse de Brabant' apart. This rose requires adequate spacing for optimum growth and bloom. It makes a great specimen plant in a perennial border and works well with three to five plants in a group in special locations. Avoid overcrowded, damp, or closed-in areas.

'Else Poulsen'—'Else Poulsen' displays wave after wave of medium-large blossoms. The distinctive upright form and bright coloration of the blossoms make the plant look like a beautiful cyclamen created for a race of giants. 'Else Poulsen' has shown tolerance to poor soils. Excellent air circulation will help reduce the incidence of disease. This selection is best suited for use in background plantings where its size and high-impact color can be used to advantage.

"Georgetown Tea"—"Georgetown Tea" is an outstanding upright, bushy found rose that has petals that roll to a point, giving each bloom a starlike appearance. It has healthy, disease-resistant, attractive foliage and works well as a mannerly specimen or in a mass or border with drifts of annuals or perennials in front. It was discovered in a Georgetown, Texas, garden by William C. Welch.

Knock Out®—This shrub rose set a new standard in disease resistance with little to no maintenance required. It has stunning flower power that provides an almost nonstop abundance of single cherry-red blossoms. Black spot resistant, drought tolerant, and self-cleaning, this rose suits every garden and every lifestyle. Knock Out® is an excellent choice for everyone, and probably the very best choice for gardeners who are just beginning with roses.

Knock Out®.

'La Marne'—'La Marne' is another older rose selection, with origins dating back to 1915. It is best known for its use as a hedge plant, reaching heights of four to six feet with a two- to three-foot spread. 'La Marne' is a very erect, bushy plant, covered with glossy leaves and loose clusters of pink and white flowers. When placed in open, sunny areas, 'La Marne' reblooms heavily in the landscape. Because of its neat, healthy, full growth and repeat bloom, 'La Marne' is a good choice for a rose hedge, especially in sunny, open areas. Of course, it is also useful as a specimen and in perennial beds.

'La Marne.'

'Madame Antoine Mari'—'Madame Antoine Mari' was named in 1901 after the wife of the breeder. This tea rose is an outstanding landscape performer reaching a height of three to five feet with a two-foot spread. The flowers consist of dark rose petals blending to pale pink. Flowers are very fragrant and their shape is similar to that of a camellia. This rose is best known for its compact habit and reflowering characteristics. It was named "Earth-Kind® Rose of the Year" for 2008 by the Texas AgriLife Extension Service.

'Madame Antoine Mari' (image courtesy of Mike Shoup).

'Monsieur Tillier'—'Monsieur Tillier' is classified as a tea rose and was first introduced in 1891. Its fully double, fragrant blossoms are an unusual orange pink and the shrub eventually attains a height and width of five to six feet. Flowers occur during all the warm months of the year and resistance to black spot is excellent. The flowers are good for cutting and the vigorous growth habit makes for a fine hedge in the landscape.

'Monsieur Tillier.'

'Mrs. Dudley Cross.'

'Mutabilis.'

"Spice" (image courtesy of Mike Shoup).

'Mrs. Dudley Cross'—'Mrs. Dudley Cross' has been a popular old tea rose since it was introduced in 1907. It is particularly abundant in the San Antonio area. A special feature is that 'Mrs. Dudley Cross' is almost thornless. It is also known for its resistance to black spot. The flowers are great for garden display or cutting. They are a lovely blend of pink and pale yellow and occur throughout the warm season. The plant grows to around five by five feet and makes an excellent large hedge. 'Mrs. Dudley Cross' was named "Earth-Kind® Rose of the Year" for 2011.

'Mutabilis'—'Mutabilis' was introduced prior to 1894. It is one of the most famous and beloved of the old garden roses. Amazing medium-sized single blossoms pass through three distinct color phases (hence the name 'Mutabilis,' since the blooms "mutate" in color), beginning with yellow, changing to pink, and finally turning to crimson. 'Mutabilis' is also known as the butterfly rose because its blossoms look like brightly colored butterflies that have landed on the bush. Named 2005 "Earth-Kind® Rose of the Year" by Texas AgriLife Extension Service, this is a large, attractive shrub that is supremely easy to grow and has great heat tolerance, making it well suited for growing in the South. Be sure to give it plenty of room to grow. It can also be pruned to form a spectacular rose tree eight to ten feet in height.

"Spice"—"Spice" produces wave after wave of blush-pink double blossoms with a peppery fragrance that probably gave rise to its name. The blooms are light pink in cooler weather to almost white in the heat of summer. Very healthy and easy to grow, "Spice" is a drought-tolerant evergreen in the South. Flowers are good for cutting and using in vases and arrangements. Arrange shrubs in a cluster of three to five plants at the back of a rose planting, or utilize as a backdrop for annuals, perennials, or herbs. "Spice" can also be grown in a large pot on your deck or patio. It is an excellent choice for everyone, especially those who are new to rose growing.

Mannerly Climbers

'Climbing Pinkie'—Having very few thorns makes 'Climbing Pinkie' the perfect rose to train on columns, trellises, and arbors. It is beautiful cascading down a rock retaining wall or along the top of a rail fence. It can even be grown trailing down a steep incline, as a large mounding shrub, or as an informal hedge. 'Climbing Pinkie' will tolerate saline irrigation water as long as there is plenty of organic matter in the soil and the irrigation water doesn't contact the foliage. Old canes should be removed after flowering has finished in late spring each year. This allows new canes to develop for next year's bloom.

'Climbing Pinkie' (image courtesy of Ralph Anderson).

'Sea Foam'—This is a rambling rose that can be used as a short climber or as ground cover. 'Sea Foam' can be the answer to embankments. Want a ground cover that you can shape a little with a pair of hedge clippers? 'Sea Foam' is the answer. The creamy white blossoms glow in the nighttime garden. For something dramatic, try 'Sea Foam' trained as a standard.

Vigorous Climbers

'New Dawn'—The Plant Patent Act of 1930 granted the breeder or discoverer of a new plant variety the right to control its propagation and distribution for seventeen years, after which it becomes common property. 'New Dawn' has historical significance because it holds the first plant patent ever granted. Double white flowers blushed with pink appear singly or in small clusters on thorny canes and produce a prolific flush of blooms in the spring. This vigorous rose has glossy foliage, great disease resistance, and tolerance of poor soil and partial shade. It is often used to train up into a tree or on a wall or sturdy trellis. The canes can be heavy and hard to work with and will require strong support, but the resulting floral display is well worth the effort.

'Sea Foam' (image courtesy of Mike Shoup).

'New Dawn.'

'Reve d'Or'—'Reve d'Or' (pronounced "rehv dohr") translates from the French as "dream of gold" or "golden dream." Its blossoms have been described as buff yellow with shades of apricot, golden

'Reve d'Or' (image courtesy of Mike Shoup).

hued, or deep yellow with shades of copper. Foliage starts out red and matures to a rich, glossy green. Blooms appear in flushes throughout the growing season with particularly lovely fall blooms. Double blossoms are medium large, with twenty-three to thirty frilly petals. They have a strong tea fragrance. The canes of this vigorous climber grow to eighteen feet. Because the canes are thin and flexible when young, they are easy to handle and can be used to nicely cover structures such as arches and pergolas. 'Reve d'Or' is nearly thornless, making it especially useful on structures where there is frequent human traffic. It strongly resents any pruning beyond shortening its vigorous summer shoots. This cultivar is so outstanding that it was named "Earth-Kind® Rose of the Year" for 2010 by the Texas AgriLife Extension Service.

ROSE RUSTLER FAVORITES

Bill Welch

'Belinda's Dream'—My son, Will, is a great guy and the father of the two most beautiful girls in the world, but he is not an enthusiastic gardener. Even so, he has grown 'Belinda's Dream' with great success.

'Climbing Cramoisi Superieur'—The image of this growing at an 1890s home in Williamsburg is firmly in my mind along with the fun I had with Peggy Cornett (a horticulturist at Monticello) in finding it and contacting the owner requesting cuttings. Anyone can create a garden picture with this rose.

"Katy Road Pink"—The toughest, best-performing rose I have ever grown.

'Marie Pavié'—Heavenly fragrance, fabulous rebloom, and compact form. What more could you ask for?

"Natchitoches Noisette"—As good as a shrub rose can get! Seeing my find being enjoyed in so many gardens is a great joy. Finding this rose and "McClinton Tea" the same day was almost overwhelming.

"Natchitoches Noisette" (image courtesy of Ralph Anderson}.

'*Old Blush*'—I have gone through periods when I thought there were better roses, but when everything about it is considered, it's about as good as a rose can be. Mike Shoup's use of an 'Old Blush' hedge bordered by cemetery white iris (*Iris × albicans*) has inspired me to re-create that combination in our own garden and many others.

"*Peggy Martin*"—Anyone can grow this rose successfully. Training it may be another matter! However, the flexible and thornless canes are a joy and really make training it less of a challenge.

'*Reve d'Or*'—Something about that apricot color and the fact that it is seldom not blooming make it an all-time favorite. Seeing it spilling over walls in the Garden District of New Orleans created lasting memories.

'*Souvenir de la Malmaison*'—Perhaps the most beautiful rose I have ever seen!

Swamp rose—Defines diversity among roses. The "weepy" form and grace of the plant along with first discovering it as such an "unassuming" plant in our North Louisiana garden give it a special place. Seeing the original plant still thriving, even though it was set out many years ago in the Native Garden at Longue Vue in New Orleans, and knowing that it survived the inundation and winds of Hurricane Katrina, puts it on my honor roll.

Swamp rose.

Greg Grant

'Belinda's Dream'—The perfect combination of a vigorous old rose and a showy new rose with large double pink flowers that everybody loves.

'Cecile Brunner'—When I was in graduate school I proposed a Valentine's Day promotion where plants of the original sweetheart rose were given to lovers as gifts that kept on giving. The delicate pink buds on this rather compact polyantha are perfect for courting. The same perfect flowers are produced on the taller spray form and climbing version as well.

'Duchesse de Brabant'—Not only is this bush tough, but the pink cupped flowers are among the most fragrant of all teas. It speaks to me!

'Enchantress'—*Southern Living* once asked me to recommend the two most disease-resistant roses, and this beautiful, compact, magenta-colored tea was one of them.

'La Marne'—I first fell for this almost single-petaled polyantha rose while working at the brand-new Antique Rose Emporium and continued to admire it in rural landscapes near Caldwell while making the long treks back and forth from East Texas to my successive jobs in San Antonio. The flower clusters occur in shades of pink and white and have a light, pleasant fragrance.

'Louis Philippe' (image courtesy of Ralph Anderson).

'Louis Philippe'—Once known as the "Creole rose" and the "Florida rose," this vigorous red China is the quintessential Southern heirloom yard rose.

'Marie Pavié'—Bill first introduced me to this polyantha rose with its powerfully fragrant clusters of white flowers. I grow the pinker sport 'Marie Daly' just behind my house.

'Monsieur Tillier'—I love all true tea roses, and all true tea roses love the South. This coral-pink beauty is a winner.

'Mrs. B. R. Cant'—This vigorous rose-colored workhorse is the other healthy gal I recommended for *Southern Living*. She's a true tea as well.

"Queenie"—I don't know this thornless once-blooming rambler's true name, but her masses of small, hot-pink flowers in the spring are stunning.

Margaret Sharpe

The late Margaret Sharpe (one of the founding members of the Texas Rose Rustlers along with Pam Puryear and Bill Welch) once mentioned these as her top ten favorites. This list was published (as is) in the 2001 winter edition of *The Old Texas Rose* but originally appeared in the 1996 November/December issue of *Texas Gardener* magazine.

Fortuniana—This white-blooming, heat-loving beauty thrives in tough conditions including dry, sandy soil. The large double flowers emit a violet fragrance. In the landscape the nearly thornless canes spread eight to ten feet. Fortuniana was discovered in China in 1850.

'Mutabilis'—The "butterfly rose" earns its common name for the five-petaled flowers that change from yellow to dark crimson as they mature. According to Margaret, 'Mutabilis' is also easy to recognize for its smooth-edged foliage. New growth is brushed with bronze. This rose grows to six feet in all directions, shrugs off disease, and, says Margaret, is tough enough to come back after freezing to the ground.

'Cramoisi Superieur'—Margaret includes this old rose because it "blooms all the time." The cup-shaped crimson flowers exude a fruity fra-

'Cramoisi Superieur.'

grance. The upright plants reach five feet tall and thrive on neglect. 'Cramoisi Superieur' was introduced in 1832. It is sometimes found in old country gardens. [I suspect Miss Margaret may actually be talking about the real 'Louis Philippe' here. —GG]

"Maggie"—This old rose, collected by Dr. William C. Welch, tops everyone's list of favorites for its large crimson blooms, heady rose scent, vigorous growth, and tough nature. Its seven-foot canes can be pruned or trained up pillars. There is always going to be a bloom on "Maggie," says Margaret.

'Souvenir de la Malmaison'—The original name "Queen of Beauty and Fragrance" describes this elegant rose. It has large, pale pink blooms, leathery foliage, and a slow-growing nature. The compact plants seldom grow more than three feet tall. Margaret suggests including the climbing sport in the garden, as well. It produces canes up to twelve feet long.

'Duchesse de Brabant—It is said that Teddy Roosevelt liked to snip a bud of this beauty for his buttonhole. As they open, the soft pink buds form into round, cupped blooms. Margaret describes this old rose as "a producer," referring to its nearly ever-blooming nature. Plants reach four to six feet tall and have apple-green foliage.

'Perle d'Or'—As if the clusters of fragrant, pink, pompon-shaped blooms weren't enough to earn 'Perle d'Or' a spot in the garden, this tough little rose blooms almost continuously, produces an abundance of apple-green foliage, and rebuffs disease. When cutting flowers to bring indoors, Margaret recommends selecting bloom clusters that include a few of the orangish buds.

'Perle d'Or' (image courtesy of Ralph Anderson).

'Cecile Brunner'—Since its introduction in 1881, the "sweetheart rose" has decorated gardens and bouquets with its classically shaped pink buds and sprays of fragrant flowers. It won a spot on Margaret's list for its adaptability to everything from poor soils to shady conditions. The bush form reaches four feet tall; the climbing selection produces canes up to twenty feet.

'**Mrs. Dudley Cross**'—Margaret describes the blooms of this thornless rose as "pale yellow with tinges of pink on the edges." It's a frequent find, she says, in old cemeteries where it thrives with no care. Even with little attention, 'Mrs. Dudley Cross' rewards growers with an ongoing stock of fragrant double flowers on plants that reach six feet tall.

'**Marechal Niel**'—This Victorian favorite decorates gardens with long, nodding stems sporting fragrant yellow blooms that appear most heavily in spring and fall. Once established, the plants grow vigorously. Because of its sensitivity to cold weather, this old rose is recommended for zone 8 or warmer.

Shannon Sherrod

Fellow East Texan Shannon Sherrod was once an extremely active rose rustler (before parenthood rustled him) and former editor of *The Old Texas Rose*. He published this top-ten list of his "Favorite (Found) Roses" in the 2000 winter edition of *The Old Texas Rose*.

"**McClinton Tea**"—It just looks and smells like an antique should to me.

"**Georgetown Tea**"—One of my most disease-free roses.

"**Maggie**"—Has Dr. Welch ever found a bad rose?

"Maggie."

"*Bermuda's Kathleen*"—Great sprays of blooms in all shades of pink.

"*Odee Pink*"—China growth habit with tea-shaped roses: two great traits that grow well together.

'*Vincent Godsif*'—Hot-pink roses so bright you have to wear shades to enjoy it.

"*Katy Road Pink*"—Plant it by a window so you can enjoy it from under the A/C while it blooms all summer.

"*Natchitoches Noisette*"—Honest, Dr. Welch didn't help me with this list.

"*Caldwell Pink*"—Lack of scent is its only weakness.

"*Smith's Parish*"—Healthy as a mule although I'm still waiting for the solid red bloom.

Audrey McMurray

Audrey was the former editor of *The Old Texas Rose*. This top-ten list appeared in the 1998 fall edition in her "Coffee with Auntie Lotte" column with this introduction: "It's a hot and humid morning. While walking through the yard, I notice ten rose bushes that survived the long, hot summer."

'*Duchesse de Brabant*'—A tea rose introduced in 1857 and one of my favorites. With little care, she bloomed all summer long and had at one time twenty-four roses on the bush.

'*Belinda's Dream*' *(1992)*—A cross between 'Tiffany' and 'Jersey Beauty.' This fast-growing shrub is upright and sturdy with few disease problems.

'*Eutin*' *(1940)*—Marketed in the past as "Rustler's Skyrocket." A very hardy shrub. One cluster is enough to fill a vase.

'*Prosperity*' *(1919)*—Very fragrant. I have a swing set in the backyard and it has just about covered the swing with beautiful clusters of pale pink flowers.

'*Madame Berkeley*'—A tea rose introduced in 1899. It is one of my

'Duchesse de Brabant' (image courtesy of Ralph Anderson).

favorites. She has been blooming all summer long. She is a big, healthy bush with salmon-pink blooms and dark green foliage.

'Abraham Darby'—An English rose by David Austin. The blossoms weren't as big as they usually are but still a pretty rose.

'General Schablikine' (1878)—It bloomed all summer long. One long, tall stem grew from the side of the bush. I put a stake to the stem and it looks like a tree rose and has been blooming all summer.

'Mutabilis' (1894)—I think every garden should have one. Mutabilis's single petals open to sulfur yellow, changing through orange to a rich pink and finally, crimson. All of these colors will often be on display at the same time. Very impressive.

'Mutabilis.'

'*Old Blush*' *(1752)*—Now that is one hardy bush. This bush has medium, semidouble, lilac-pink petals and a delightful scent.

'*Souvenir de la Malmaison*'—This Bourbon rose was introduced in 1843. Her quartered blossoms are large and flat, with pale pink petals and a delightful scent.

Mitzi VanSant

Mitzi was one of the early Texas Rose Rustlers and probably the only one who was well versed in historical old roses when she moved from Washington State to Austin in 1979. She was south-central coordinator for the Heritage Roses Group until she moved to California in 1991. She now grows old-fashioned plants, including sixty different antique roses, around her 1929 bungalow in Smithville, Texas. She does residential landscape design under her company name, The Fragrant Garden.

"*Darlow's Enigma*" *(found rose)*—Found by Mike Darlow of Seattle, Washington. Tall, loose shrub or can be trained as a climber to about twelve feet or more. Single white blossoms are produced constantly from March through December. Fragrant. Tiny red hips in fall if blooms are not dead-headed. Available only from Heirloom Roses in Oregon.

'*Elie Beauvillain*' *(climbing tea)*—This rose is a very vigorous climber that reblooms well and carries its fragrant, medium-pink flowers at nearly every leaf axil. I have had best success with training it laterally in fan shape on a fence, but it also works on a tall trellis or arbor. Cleo Barnwell gave me this rose. She got it from Elizabeth Lawrence of Chapel Hill, North Carolina. I gave it to Mike Shoup many years ago and he returned it to the trade in Texas.

"*Maggie*" *(found rose, probably a Bourbon)*—Forms a five- to six-foot shrub, often but not constantly in flower, with large, cherry-red buds that open to cupped and quartered, many-petaled flowers. It is one of my most fragrant roses. The only thing that limits this rose is its mild propensity to black spot.

'*Marechal Niel*' *(tea Noisette climber)*—I have carried this climbing rose from Texas to California to Oregon and back to Texas again. The large buttery yellow blooms hang pendent over one of the seven large metal arbors in my garden. It doesn't repeat as well as some of my other climbers, but the color and scent make it worth it. Cold tender.

'*Mlle. Cecile Brunner*' *(polyantha)*—I have a love of all things minia-

'Mlle. Cecile
Brunner.'

'Reve d'Or' (image
courtesy of Mike
Shoup).

ture (jam jars, vases, etc.), and this tiny, pearl-pink rose is one of them. As a landscape designer who loves old roses, I put a signature rose bush in all my projects. I often select this variety, especially if there are children in the household. It has the strength of scent of a much larger rose and is almost always in bloom.

'Monsieur Tillier' (tea)—This rose forms a very large bush or can be trained as a climber over an arbor. Because of its tea heritage, it is almost always in flower. The intricate blooms are a blend of deep pink with an orangey cast in the center. Good scent.

'Reve d'Or' (Noisette climber)—This is my most remontant climbing rose, bearing apricot buds fading to creamy apricot-yellow blooms. Good scent, easily trained to fence or arbor.

'Safrano' (tea)—Another tea that makes a very large bush with regular repeat of bloom. Light but heavenly scent and the color of palest peach flushed

with white. I also love it because it is one of the most frequently mentioned roses in the literature of the old Southern gardens.

'Souvenir del la Malmaison' (Bourbon)—Blush pink, fat in bud, blossoms open cupped and quartered. Very fragrant but does get some black spot. Good but not constant rebloom. The white sport 'Kronprinzessin Viktoria' is similar in all ways except white in color.

'William R. Smith' (tea)—This rose makes a large, rounded shrub with red-tinged new foliage and large white blossoms that nod on the stem. The buds are white with a pink edge and open to many-petaled white blooms. Fragrant, and almost always the first rose to bloom in my garden and the last to give up in fall. Disease-free.

Peggy Martin

Peggy is president of the New Orleans Old Garden Rose Society and vice president and treasurer of the Heritage Rose Foundation. She is also the old garden rose and shrub chairperson for the Gulf District American Rose Society and the original source of the legendary "Peggy Martin" rose.

'LeVesuve' (China, 1825)—Very impressed with this rose again, had it in old garden too. It blooms constantly even in hottest summer months, beautiful glossy dark green foliage almost like a camellia. Color is dramatic shades of lilac pink with swirls of darker pink within the fully double flowers.

'Parade' (1953, big climber)—This is another rose that does not stop blooming in the hottest months, most impressive large double flowers, fragrant and a rich magenta pink. It grows vigorously to fifteen feet, with glossy healthy leaves, always in bloom.

'Madame Isaac Pereire' (Bourbon, 1881)—Gorgeous, rich, deep rose perfume and color of magenta, so many petals, I had one in the old garden, weighed a pound. Glossy dark green large leaves, I love this rose semipegged. Its extravagant beauty and fragrance is quintessentially perfection in a rose.

'Zephirine Drouhin' (Bourbon, 1868)—The thornless canes are so healthy with dark green foliage, large, very fragrant fuchsia blooms with fully double high centers. Exquisite!

'Zephirine Drouhin.'

'Devoniensis' (image courtesy of Peggy Martin).

'Baronne Henriette de Snoy' (tea, 1897)—Very full, quartered light pink inner and darker pink outer, long-stemmed scented flowers with a very interesting configuration of inner petals. The large, glossy, dark green, healthy leaves look like a camellia.

'Devoniensis' (tea, 1886)—So beautiful with pink buds that hold the color until fully open, then are creamy white, fully double large blossoms with fruity sweet scent covering the long, fifteen- to eighteen-foot canes, which I semipeg between the other roses surrounding it. Very impressive, also known as the magnolia rose.

'White Climbing Maman Cochet' (tea, 1907)—Large, very heavily petaled white blooms blushing on edges to pale lilac pink. Very vigorous growth with dark green healthy foliage.

'Maman Cochet' (tea, 1893)—Classic long-budded soft pink tea rose with soft yellow at base of large full blossoms. Few thorns with dark green leathery foliage.

'Perle des Jardins' (tea, 1874)—When I saw a vase of these beautiful, perfect, soft canary-yellow flowers on long, stiff stems, I knew I had to have it! Very full, fragrant flowers with dark green foliage.

'Frau Karl Druschki' (hybrid perpetual, 1901)—Gorgeous, large, pure white blooms, very full with high-centered buds, glossy and very dark green foliage, again like a camellia.

Cynthia W. Mueller

Although raised in California near the Huntington Botanical Gardens, Cynthia is a longtime Texas Master Gardener, garden writer, and volunteer in the Texas AgriLife Extension horticulture office at Texas A&M University. She had the benefit of being friends with and plant rustling with the late Pam Puryear. Cynthia specializes in Texas-tough bulbs and maintains a large crinum collection among her self-propagated roses and other eclectic babies in College Station, Texas.

"Highway 290 Pink Buttons"—I've always liked miniatures, and this is evidently one of the very first, thought to be derived from *Rosa chinensis minima*. Especially in the spring, blooms can almost cover the waist-high

"Highway 290 Pink Buttons."

bush. Flowers are pink and range from a little finger to a thumb in size. Has been found throughout the Central Texas area.

Green rose—A green sport of *Rosa chinensis viridiflora* that has a long and complicated history. It is not a "green rose" with the shape of a small hybrid tea, but a bristly mass of shaggy green sepals/tepals almost the size of a golf ball when grown under good conditions. It's found growing in gardens all around the warmer portions of the United States and does well in our heat and humidity. Amazing to think that all the plants in existence are cuttings from one original.

'Louis Philippe'—This is certainly a well-traveled red rose and seems to be found in all warm-weather areas, especially those associated with the sea travel of earlier times. I have seen it thriving in neglect beside an ancient small chapel made of white wooden boards in the country on the island of Lanai, as well as in Costa Rica and throughout the southern United States.

'Pink Grootendorst'—This rose has the health and vigor we associate with rugosas. Although rugosas are excellent for colder areas, it is extremely durable and can easily grow in southern coastal areas even in the path of salt-laden sea winds. Blooms are small pink rosettes with somewhat notched petals, produced intermittently throughout the growing season. Companion "Grootendorst" roses are 'Red Grootendorst' and 'Grootendorst Supreme.'

'Paul Neyron.'

'Old Blush'—There may be hundreds or thousands of newer pink roses, but 'Old Blush' is a standout for warm areas in terms of almost continuous flowering and the ability to create a mass of pink blooms that can be seen from over in the next block. The climbing form can create an even more noticeable display.

'Paul Neyron'—This is a hybrid perpetual shrub rose created in 1869 that was such a sensation that a color was named after her: "Neyron rose." It's still considered to have one of the largest rose flowers, six inches in diameter and crammed with petals, and it is almost thornless.

'Mrs. Dudley Cross'—This is an old-fashioned tea rose that is excellent for tough conditions and low water requirements. The chest-high shrub can be covered periodically with yellow/white classic cupped blooms tinged with pink toward the petal tips. I always admired these in old gardens on the back streets of San Antonio, where plants are rarely tossed aside in favor of newer varieties. Those that clung to hard, dry, sloped ground performed almost as well as those pampered in well-tended flower beds.

'Mlle. Cecile Brunner'—Another small favorite polyantha I remember from earliest childhood. It is always in bloom, and I enjoy growing this as well as its close relative 'Bloomfield Abundance,' which differs only in producing entire masses of small flowers from one stem, each of which can be a complete bouquet. The flower may be described as a salmon-pink, rosette-shaped "buttonhole rose."

'Pink Rosette'—This rose is said to be the result of crossing two seedlings of 'Mlle. Cecile Brunner'—but what a change was made! 'Pink Rosette' has splendid erect clusters of perfect, shell-like, medium-pink flowers a bit over one inch in diameter. When cut, they dry well after being packed in silica or sand. Plants usually do not grow above three feet in height.

'Madame Isaac Pereire'—One of the most fragrant roses, this Bourbon often grows to shoulder height. It flowers on and off through the season, but

the fall seems to be its best time. The quartered flowers are crammed with petals and can be from three to six inches in diameter, depending on the situation. The color is a rich pink that goes well with almost everything.

Leo Watermeier

Leo is a founding member of the New Orleans Old Garden Rose Society and curator of the roses in Louis Armstrong Park. He was a judge in the International Rose Trials at Bagatelle in Paris in 2009 and organizes an annual tour to public and private rose gardens in Italy. He has spoken about the old roses of New Orleans to clubs in Dallas, Houston, New York, and other cities.

'Le Pactole' (tea, pre-1845)—Clusters of bone-white flowers with a lemony scent. Healthy foliage and an excellent repeat boomer. Some consider it a Noisette.

'Le Vesuve' (tea, 1825)—Probably the best bloomer with the healthiest foliage in our hot, humid summers. Very thorny and grows into an interesting sprawling shape if left unpruned.

"Spice" (China, Bermuda found)—Similar to 'Ducher' but flowers larger, more fragrant, and less prone to powdery mildew.

'Madame Carnot' (Noisette, 1889)—Light pink, long-lasting blooms, great for cutting. Healthy foliage and excellent repeat blooming. Grows more like a moderate tea than a Noisette.

'Madame Isaac Pereire' (image courtesy of Cynthia Mueller).

'Le Vesuve' (image courtesy of Peggy Martin).

'*Marie Van Houtte*' *(tea, 1871)*—Ivory flowers tinged with pink on a lush-growing plant. Only for those with enough space, as it resents frequent heavy pruning.

'*Marie d'Orleans*' *(tea, 1883)*—Pink flowers with unusual quill-shaped petals. Mannerly grower with healthy foliage and good repeat blooms that hold up in summer heat.

'*Climbing Lady Hillingdon*' *(climbing tea, 1917)* —Much better than the shrub form. The bright apricot flowers are fuller and longer lasting.

'*St. David*' *(China, Bermuda found)*—My favorite of the small-growing, red-flowered Chinas.

'*General Gallieni*' *(tea, 1899)*—Striking, deep red flowers, almost tinged with black. Healthy foliage, good repeat blooming, and moderate growth habit.

'*Mary Washington*' *(Noisette, pre-1900)*—The most fragrant of the Noisettes. Large clusters of very pale pink flowers. Good repeat blooming.

SOURCES FOR ANTIQUE ROSES

Chamblee's Rose Nursery (retail and mail order)
> 10926 U.S. Highway 69 North
> Tyler, Texas 75706-5933
> 1-800-256-ROSE (7673)
> chambleeroses.com

Heirloom Roses (mail order)
> 24062 NE Riverside Drive
> St. Paul, Oregon 97137
> 1-800-820-0465
> heirloomroses.com

Petals from the Past (retail and mail order)
> 16034 County Road 29
> Jemison, Alabama 35085
> 205-646-0069
> petalsfromthepast.com

The Antique Rose Emporium (retail and mail order)
> 10,000 FM 50
> Brenham (Independence), Texas 77833
> 1-800-441-0002
> antiqueroseemporium.com

The Arbor Gate Nursery (retail)
> 15635 FM 2920
> Tomball, Texas 77377
> 281-351-8851
> arborgate.com

The Arbor Gate Nursery, Tomball, Texas. Specialty nurseries across the South continue to supply a wide variety of adapted roses to gardeners.

MORE INFORMATION

Organizations

Texas Rose Rustlers
texasroserustlers.com

Heritage Rose Foundation
P.O. Box 831414
Richardson, Texas 75083
heritagerosefoundation.org

Southern Garden History Society
P.O. Box 15752
Winston-Salem, North Carolina 27113
336-770-6723
southerngardenhistory.org

Books

Antique Roses for the South (2004, William C. Welch)
Empress of the Garden (2013, G. Michael Shoup)
Heirloom Gardening in the South (2011, William C. Welch and Greg Grant)
In Search of Lost Roses (2002, Tom Christopher)
Landscaping with Antique Roses (1992, Liz Druitt and G. Michael Shoup)
Mystery Roses around the World (2011, Heritage Rose Foundation)
Noisette Roses: 19th Century Charleston's Gift to the World (2010, Virginia
    Kean, editor)
Old Rose Survivors–Wild and Untamed (2014, Heritage Rose Foundation)
Once Upon a Time...A Cemetery Story (2009, Jane White)
Perennial Garden Color (1989, William C. Welch)
Roses in Bermuda Revisited (2013, Bermuda Rose Society)
The Organic Rose Garden (2004, Liz Druitt)

INDEX